Creating Striking Graphics with Maya and Photoshop

Creating Striking Graphics with Maya® and Photoshop®

Daniel Gray

San Francisco • London

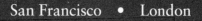

SYBEX®

Associate Publisher: Dan Brodnitz
Alias Learning Tools and Training Product Manager:
    Danielle Lamothe
Acquisitions and Developmental Editor: Mariann Barsolo
Alias Acquisitions Editor: Erica Fyvie
Production Editor: Elizabeth Campbell
Technical Editor: Keith Reicher
Copyeditor: Pat Coleman
Compositor: Side by Side Studios
CD Coordinator: Dan Mummert
CD Technician: Kevin Ly
Proofreaders: Rachel Gunn, Lori Newman, Laurie O'Connell,
    Nancy Riddiough
Indexer: Ted Laux
Book Designer: Mark Ong, Side by Side Studios
Cover Designer: Louis Fishauf
Alias Global Package Services Product Development Manager:
    Carla Sharkey

To Debbie, Ali, and Colt … you make it all worth doing.

Acknowledgments

At Sybex, a mountain of thanks to my fabulous Acquisitions and Developmental Editor Mariann Barsolo, Associate Publisher Dan Brodnitz, Production Editor Elizabeth Campbell, Technical Editor Keith Reicher, Copyeditor Pat Coleman, Book Designer Mark Ong, and Compositors Mark Ong and Susan Riley of Side by Side Studios for all their hard work.

At Alias, many thanks to Danielle Lamothe, Erica Fyvie, Carla Sharkey, and Michael Stamler. And at Adobe, many thanks to John Nack.

Thanks to Louis Fishauf for his beautiful cover design, which showcases Meats Meier's *Mother Nature* so well.

Thanks to Dariush Derakhshani for his fine work on Chapters 2 and 3.

To all of the artists and studios that contributed to this book … there wouldn't be a book without your incredible artwork and support:

Marc-André Guindon for his amazing work with the Tiki Terminals. Thank you kindly for your great modeling, texturing, lighting, and rendering efforts.

Meats Meier, for sticking with me while the *Hellboy* fires raged. Each time I look at *Mother Nature* I see something new.

At guru studios, Frank Falcone, Holly Nichols, Ben Mazzotta, Barry Sanders, and Max Piersig for your time and insight into the innovative guru process. A great cartoon is a great cartoon, no matter what the medium.

Damon Riesberg, for being so patient and informative over the months in which your chapter took shape. I have faith that one day the *Syntax Errors* kids will run in the Sunday funnies, nationwide.

At Meteor Studios, Christine LeClerc, Chloe Grysole, Isabelle Riva, Francois Garcia for the incredible in-depth look at how the Orodromeus came to life. I'll never look at a dinosaur the same way again.

At IBM's e-business Innovation Center, Colin Freeman and John Tolva for working with me while the deadlines loomed from across the globe. The work of your crew will enable generations to see into the past.

Michael Elins for spending so much time to ensure that the story was spot on. Your work is an inspiration. Linas Jodwalis for his excellent insight and support.

At Meshwerks, Kevin Scheidle for instantly digging the EleMENTAL Woodie idea and for all your wonderful support, Dave Owen for your awesome work on the Woodie, Keith Johnston and GTN for their terrific rendering.

Thanks to Mirko Ilić and Lauren DeNapoli for working with me under tight deadlines to create an absolutely stunning chapter.

And to Mark Bamforth and Al Ward for their help with research and writing.

Dariush would like to thank Dell Computers and Matt Ceniceros for their continued support and well-built workstations. Also, thanks to Randi Munn for her help with the wine bottle labels in Chapter 3.

Letter from the Publisher

Dear Reader,

Thank you for choosing *Creating Striking Graphics with Maya and Photoshop*. This book is part of the growing library of Sybex graphics books, all written by outstanding authors— artists and teachers who really know their stuff and have a clear vision of the audience they're writing for.

Founded in 1976, Sybex is the oldest independent computer book publisher. More than twenty-five years later, we're committed to producing a full line of consistently exceptional graphics books. With each title, we're working hard to set a new standard for the industry. From the paper we print on, to the writers and photographers we work with, our goal is to bring you the best graphics books available.

I hope you see all that reflected in these pages. I'd be very interested to hear your comments and get your feedback on how we're doing. To let us know what you think about this or any other Sybex book, please visit us at www.sybex.com. Once there, go to the book's page, click on Submit Feedback, and fill out the questionnaire. Your input is greatly appreciated.

Please also visit www.sybex.com to learn more about the rest of our graphics line.

Best regards,

Dan Brodnitz
Associate Publisher—Graphics
Sybex Inc.

Foreword

When it comes down to it, it's all about the subject. As artists, we strive to create the most compelling, memorable, and unique visual experiences we can. Every day, we challenge ourselves to leave a lasting impact on our audiences. The process of creating, despite the occasional pain it brings, is always absorbing and gratifying.

In the past, our task was more straightforward. It was never simple, but it was less complicated. We had to create something beautiful that would exist within the boundaries of a page. It had to look great printed, and it had to capture the reader's attention and hold it long enough that the message came across. While those requirements are still as critical today, I believe we are heading towards the additional challenge of creating something that can resonate within a variety of media. Where we might once have had control over the presentation of the printed images, we will also have to contend with the requirements of the web or other digital formats.

Today, you may need to create an image for print, and then animate it for the web or translate it to video. Each experience is different and unique in its own way and is not to be discounted. How do we take advantage of that uniqueness to create as compelling an experience as possible regardless of whether we are looking at a still image or an animation? It was this challenge that introduced me to the world beyond two dimensions, beyond the tools of photography and Photoshop that I'd been using. I wanted to produce the kinds of images that I was seeing in my head, and then, I wanted to see them move! Collaborating with various Maya artists has opened up the third dimension for me and, as such, the world of possibilities—I'm excited to explore them all.

I was eager to participate in this book because I see this marriage of 2D and 3D as essential to the future of our craft. As we continue to strive to surprise and delight our audiences, we will need to consider all of the potential media through which our creative visions can be displayed. You'll see many examples in these pages of graphic artists who are achieving results that would once have been impossible. These examples cross all of the potential media where our images live: television, web, film, print, virtual dioramas, comic strips, product design, photography and illustration. I encourage you to explore these options and not be left behind.

Michael Elins
www.michaelelins.com

About the Authors

Daniel Gray is a writer, designer, and life-long resident of the Garden State. For close to fifteen years, Dan has specialized in the topic of computer graphics. Writing from the designer's perspective, his books have been successful worldwide, having been translated into ten languages. Brazil and the Netherlands have been two of Dan's best international markets over the years. (*Inside CorelDRAW!* was a #1 computer book best-seller in Brazil.) With his son Colt's great ability in the world's sport of soccer, Dan hopes to visit both those countries one day.

Dariush Derakhshani is an effects animator and educator in Los Angeles, California. Previously using CAD software in his architecture days, Dariush migrated to using 3D programs when his firm's principle architects needed to show their clients design work on the computer. Starting with Alias PowerAnimator version 6, when he enrolled in USC Film School's Animation program, Dariush has been using Alias animation software for the past nine years. From USC, he received an MFA in Film, Video and Computer Animation in 1997. Dariush also holds a BA in Architecture and Theatre from Lehigh University in Pennsylvania and worked at a New Jersey architecture firm before moving to LA for film school. Dariush has worked on feature films, music videos and countless commercials as a 3D animator, CG lead, and sometimes compositor.

Contents

Chapter 11   Mirko Ilić: A Body of Work in 3D   181

Introduction

Welcome to *Creating Striking Graphics with Maya and Photoshop* and the cutting edge of photo-realistic and surrealistic design. If you're a Photoshop artist coming to this book, sit back and enjoy the ride. The intent of the book is not to overwhelm you with technical details, but to help ease you into the world of Maya through exciting designs and real-world stories. In the following chapters, you'll see the innovative techniques that artists are using to expand their capabilities, win new clients, and create an entirely new genre of art. If you're already a Maya artist, you'll enjoy reading about and be inspired by the work being produced with the combination of these two highly-powerful tools.

As electronic artists, we share a common ground in the quest to expand our boundaries. Straight out, there's nothing that provides a world without boundaries like the combination of Maya and Adobe Photoshop. Inspiration should not be constrained by limitations, whether real or perceived. An idea should be allowed to develop independently of the software and hardware you use. Your vision must be allowed its freedom. Your mind's eye must be allowed to connect to what can develop inside the computer… and it all must happen through transference between your brain and the greatest graphics software on the planet.

What You will Learn from this Book

Creating Striking Graphics with Maya and Photoshop is not your average computer how-to book. While it has a certain how-to aspect, the lion's share of the book seeks to demonstrate how-we-did-it. Some of the early chapters are focused on some pertinent, specific information on Maya and how it works with Photoshop. Most of the chapters tell the stories and provide details on artists that have taken the leap to 3D.

Through lavish full-color illustrations, you'll see how the artists tackled the job of re-creating ancient worlds and creatures, hilarious cartoons and comic strips, and exquisite editorial illustrations alike.

Who Should Read this Book

Any Photoshop artist thinking about entering the world of 3D will benefit from reading this book. Learning about how Maya and Photoshop work together through the eyes of the artists that have already taken the leap will afford valuable insight into the capabilities of this absolutely incredible program.

And for folks that have already taken up the Maya torch, this book will help you see how your colleagues have made the leap from 2D to 3D. Whether you need a leg up, or an inspirational push, *Creating Striking Graphics with Maya and Photoshop* will prove itself to be a valuable companion.

How This Book is Organized

Creating Striking Graphics with Maya and Photoshop consists of two main parts. Part 1 lays the groundwork to get you familiar with the world of 3D design, so that you more fully understand the potential of integrating Maya and Photoshop. Part 2 delves into case studies of the artists and studios that are changing the face of design, through their expert use of these two powerful programs.

Part 1: Maya and Photoshop: A Beautiful Friendship

Need the groundwork to understand the hows and whys of Maya and Photoshop? Part 1 will get you off on the right foot, as it provides examples and explanations.

Chapter 1 In this chapter, the ball gets rolling with a (sur)real-world example of why you might to use Maya and Photoshop together to build images for a mythical marketing campaign. You'll learn how the marvelous Internet-connected Tiki terminal came to be, and why we decided to chop the top of a Honda Element and turn it into a not-so-old-fashioned woodie wagon: the EleMENTAL Woodie.

Chapter 2 Maya expert Dariush Derakhshani provides some of the 3D technology basics as they apply to Maya, and for working with Maya and Photoshop together.

Chapter 3 This time, Dariush gives you a couple of quick hands-on exercises to familiarize you with the ways artists use Maya and Photoshop in concert to create images.

Part 2: Striking Graphics for Various Markets

Part 2 provides eight chapters that are chock-full of amazing artwork and marvelous insight into the minds of the artists and inner-workings of the studios that are using Maya and Photoshop to crank out cutting-edge world-class artwork.

Chapter 4 Named a Maya Master in 2003, Meats Meier enjoys a fine reputation in the world of 3D art. Meats's printed work has graced the pages and covers of many a magazine. In this chapter, you'll learn how Meats uses Maya and Photoshop together to create his striking series of Mother Nature images.

Chapter 5 guru studios has a mission to bring the time-honored art and principles of traditional cartoon animation into the world of 3D. Their work harkens back to the classic age of Warner Brothers cartoons, propelling their pieces into a fabulously funny realm. In this chapter, you'll see how guru studios created a marvelous series of bumper animations for the Canadian TELETOON network.

Chapter 6 Damon Riesberg's day job as an animator with PDI/Dreamworks has him working on feature films like *Shrek 2*. At night, he produces his own comic strip, *Syntax Errors*. Rest assured, *Syntax Errors* isn't a normal comic strip … it's produced entirely in Maya and Photoshop. In this chapter, you'll learn how the process of posing and rendering replaces the age-old technique of drawing and redrawing, with Damon's streamlined comic strip production pipeline. If the great Charles Schultz were alive today, he'd be reading this chapter.

Chapter 7 Meteor Studios specializes in breathing life into a wide range of animated subjects for the Discovery Channel and other media outlets. This chapter documents some of the painstaking work done to create their Visual Effects Society Award Nominated feature, *Dinosaur Planet*. You'll learn how Meteor imparts such amazing realism to their prehistoric creatures, through a thorough dissection of the North American Orodromeus.

Chapter 8 Acclaimed fine artist and photo-illustrator Michael Elins uses a combination of Photoshop and Maya to produce editorial artwork for a range of publications including *The New York Times Sunday Magazine, Time, Newsweek,* and *Vanity Fair.* While Michael is an expert Photoshop user, he has chosen not to use Maya himself, preferring to partner with Maya experts as he creates a whole new genre of art that honors the classic techniques while embracing the new technology.

Chapter 9 IBM's e-business Innovation Center in Atlanta, Georgia uses Maya and Photoshop to re-create Egyptian architecture and artifacts in a complex interactive installation for the Egyptian Museum in Cairo, Egypt. Media Director Colin Freeman's 3D team literally built cities from the ground up, showing a progression over time to offer an experience unrivaled in its interactive nature. Museum and Web visitors get to walk through and fly by the ancient worlds, as never before.

Chapter 10 Meshwerks has the automotive enthusiasts dream job: they get to digitize the world's newest and coolest cars, creating high-end 3D models that are used in motion pictures, video games, and advertising. In this chapter, you'll see how Meshwerks digitized the very first Ford GT supercar off the assembly line and learn the details of how Meshwerks turned a mundane SUV into the ultra-cool chopped and lowered Honda EleMENTAL Woodie. Get out your torches and reciprocating saws … this chapter's cooler than an episode of *Monster Garage!*

Chapter 11 From his New York City-based studio, Mirko Ilić has spent the past decade producing an amazing array of 3D artwork. This chapter consists of a gallery that showcases some of Mirko's most brilliant pieces. The studio's collaborative workflow ensures total creative freedom while meeting a torrid pace of deadlines in the world of editorial art and graphic design.

Hardware and Software Considerations

Maya runs on four distinct operating systems—Windows 2000/XP, Irix, Linux, and Mac OS X—so specifying which particular hardware components will work with Maya is a challenge. To help you out, Alias has a "qualified hardware" page on their website that describes the latest hardware qualified to work with Maya for each operating system. Go to this URL:

    http://www.alias.com/eng/support/maya/qualified_hardware/index.jhtml

Although there are specific hardware recommendations on these web pages, we can offer you some general information to consider when you are preparing to run Maya. First, be sure to get a fast processor; Maya goes through CPU cycles quickly, so this one is important. Next, you need plenty of RAM (memory) to run Maya; 512MB is a minimum, but 1GB is advisable, especially if you are working with large scene files.

Also, if you want to be able to interact within your Maya scenes, you'll need a powerful video card. Maya will work with a poor graphics card, but screen redraws will be painfully slow in complex scenes, and you may find yourself very frustrated. For the best performance, you may rather go with a "workstation graphics card" than a consumer-grade gaming video card. There is a variety of workstation cards for different levels of perform-ance, so you should be able to find one in your price range. It's important to also have a large hard disk, but this is only a concern if you are trying to use Maya on an older computer, as current computers come with more than enough space.

Here are some suggested setups (current at the time of writing):

- Windows or Linux
  - AMD Athlon XP 2400+; 1GB RAM; ATI FireGL X1; 160GB hard disk
  - Intel Pentium IV 2.8GHz; 1GB RAM; nVidia Quadro FX1100; 160GB 7200rpm hard disk
- Mac OS X
  - PowerMac G5 dual 1.25GHz; 1GB RAM; ATI Radeon 9800pro Mac Edition; 160GB hard disk, third-party three-button mouse
- Irix
  - Silicon Graphics Octane 2; dual 600MHz; 1GB RAM; built-in graphics; 80GB hard disk

With the current speed of computer hardware, many laptop computers can run Maya comfortably as well. Additionally, even hardware that is not officially supported by Alias can often run Maya—just remember that you will not be able to get technical support if your system does not meet Alias's qualifications chart.

The Book's CD

The CD in the back of this book provides all of the sample images, movies, and files that you need to work through the tutorial in Chapter 3, as well as Maya Personal Learning Edition.

Related files on the CD are indicated with the CD icon in the margin. The CD accom-panying this book has been tested on Windows, Mac, and Linux machines and should work with most configurations of these systems.

Maya Personal Learning Edition

If you don't already have a version of Maya, you might want to install the Maya Personal Learning Edition (Maya PLE) software, which you can find on the CD at the back of this book. Maya PLE is a special version of Maya that gives you free access to Maya Complete for noncommercial use. Maya PLE works on Windows 2000/XP Professional and Mac OS X.

Website For This Book

You can find updated information about this book and provide us with feedback at www.sybex.com. You may also find a random array of thoughts and other juicy tidbits (includ-ing updates on the fabulous EleMENTAL Woodie and Tiki Terminals) at the author's web-site: www.geekbooks.com.

Contact the Author

You can contact Daniel Gray at mayapshop@geekbooks.com.

one

PART

Maya and Photoshop: A Beautiful Friendship

The combination of Maya and Photoshop presents the graphic artist with an unlimited realm of creative possibilities. The latest versions of these programs take this software camaraderie to a whole new level. Enhanced interaction between the programs provides a workflow that speeds up the creative process, while allowing rapid revisions and limitless creative freedom.

one

Drawing a New Course in a 3D World

Daniel Gray

At its basic premise, *this book seeks to open your mind to the world of possibilities when designing with Maya and Photoshop. To that end, put aside your current design capabilities, and think how life might be if your images were not constrained by two dimensions, by your illustration skills, or by the depth of your photo library. The combination of Maya and Photoshop present the graphic artist with the opportunity to expand beyond the limitations of the real world, to knock down the tired old walls and build beautiful new palaces of creative expression. By cutting the restraints, the addition of Maya to your creative toolbox will open up your world, allowing you to push forward into a place you've never been; a place where anything is possible.*

Let's Work Together

Maya and Photoshop have a symbiotic relationship. Although they are very different programs, they complement each other well. For example, you can create textures entirely in Maya, or you can bring them in from Photoshop. Scene lighting is largely handled in Maya, but you might tweak certain effects in the final render by working on it into Photoshop. All in all, complete images and individual components move back and forth between the two programs with great regularity. As an example, in Chapter 4, you'll learn how multiple renders from Maya can be assembled in a layered Photoshop file, to create the most highly detailed images for print. And in Chapter 7, you'll learn how UV mappings are exported from Maya into Photoshop, where you can easily paint and modify them before bringing them back into Maya. With the ability to create layered Photoshop files added in Maya 6, your creative possibilities are increased exponentially.

Maya 6 provides an enhanced workflow to and from Photoshop. This latest version of Maya reads and writes native Photoshop PSD files. Through this tight integration, you can fully explore your layered textures in Photoshop, with the PSD file directly linked to your Maya model. This provides a straightforward texturing and painting methodology. With the support of the Photoshop PSD format (version 6 and later), simple painting workflows allow for the following:

- The use of any Photoshop file as a Maya texture
- The instant update of Photoshop-modified PSD files within Maya, upon refresh
- The conversion of layered PSD files to Maya layered textures
- The construction of layered PSD files from Maya, thus allowing you to paint an object's color, bump, and specular channels separately in Photoshop
- The creation of "lipstick" sketches in Maya, using the 3D Paint tool, thus allowing you to create a guideline object for painting within Photoshop

Lipstick sketches are especially helpful to show Photoshop artists where to paint. This method is best used when you have a model with UVs that lack sufficient direction for the artist to follow. (You might think of it as painting between the lines when the lines would not otherwise be visible.)

Photoshop artists can apply their existing skills to Maya in a number of ways. Here are just a handful of examples:

Wilder Than the Wildest Thing If the real object is not available, you can create (or re-create) it (as you'll see in the following examples and throughout the book).

Stairway to 3D Heaven You can push the limits of the real world by combining 3D models with photographic images to create convincing mockups.

Born to Revise Once a 3D model is created, you can animate it, recolor it, retexture it, relight it, rotate it, resize it, and reposition it to your heart's content, thus allowing for complete flexibility. "You want a green suit? Bring in the green light."

Pop's Not Just for Music Painting textures on a 3D model can lift your images off the page by adding amazing detail and depth to your graphic designs.

Buy a Model or Just Look Like One You can purchase 3D models to jump-start your designs. Need some furniture or a specific vehicle? Cool. Need to modify that furniture or vehicle? Even cooler.

If you are purely a Photoshop artist at present, your career can only benefit from expanding your knowledge and capabilities. The precedent has been set by the motion picture and video game industries. There is no turning back. Our audience expects nothing less than magic, and as artists we must learn how to make that magic or face a career change. Now that might seem extreme to some, but take a look back to see how far the field of graphic design and illustration has come in the past 20 years since the advent of the Macintosh.

At present, learning 3D or Maya—or at least learning how to incorporate Maya into your work—will allow you to break away from your less adventurous competition. The expansion of the medium is a given. We're doing things today that have never been done before. Tomorrow, we'll be doing things that we can't dream of today. For those who feel we have moved mountains so far, we'll soon be moving entire planets.

If you've given some thought to learning Maya and entering the world of 3D, this first chapter will give you just a taste of what's possible at the infinite buffet. Although the world of 3D can seem intimidating to the 2D artist, it needn't be. You can go about it two ways: learn Maya yourself, or collaborate with a Maya artist.

If learning 3D seems too time-consuming in your busy life, at least consider incorporating 3D into your 2D graphic illustration world. By collaborating with Maya artists, you put your toe in the water and add depth to your portfolio. But you may find that once you've had a taste, you'll want to begin exploring Maya on your own.

In that spirit, we're going to show you how having Maya available in your tool palette gives you artistic freedom and new, exciting challenges as well. Chapter 2 will provide more information on the basic concepts of 3D, as well as detail the way that Maya and Photoshop work together. But for now, we'll start with a mock project that's sure to stretch any artist's imagination.

Maya and Photoshop Walk into a Bar ...

To illustrate working with Maya and Photoshop, I took on my own project. I was looking for an example of how a 3D workflow might enhance the creative possibilities of a Photoshop artist. Although this fictional job might seem a bit over the top, that is its intent.

Let's say I have been called on to help with a marketing campaign pitch for a hotel chain that's looking to launch a string of Tiki bars at their resorts. "Oh, wow," I think to myself, "a Tiki bar."

Now *that's* not so original, right? But the more I look into the subject, the deeper I'm drawn into the research. And as always, the Web provides a wealth of reference material and endless inspiration. Newly fascinated with the world of Tikis, I embark on a quest to research the art of Tiki-making, frittering away many hours browsing the Tiki-wares listed on eBay and other fabulous websites such as tikifarm.com. In fact, it's the Tiki Farm that draws me in with the promise of a seemingly endless supply of unique and wonderful Tiki mugs and other supplies (see Figure 1.1). So I called the Tiki Farm and asked for permission to use their fabulous Tiki bar as inspiration for this piece.

Figure 1.1: The Tiki Farm website

Creating a Tiki Bar

The hotel marketing squad wants their new string of Tiki bars to make a huge splash, and they're willing to consider some really wild and different approaches to marketing. They want state-of-the-art, Internet-equipped dens of frozen cocktail indulgence. Polynesian kitsch meets the wired age. As the designer, I'm faced with a splendid dilemma: how can I work Internet terminals into a Tiki bar? How can I not only pull it off, but make it really cool?

After a considerable number of ideas are thrown into and dumped out of the creative blender, I came up with *the* idea: build the Internet terminals *into Tikis* ... that's right ... the world's first Tiki Net terminals!

Creating a Tiki Terminal

Corporate management has decided that the Tiki terminal will be one of the main highlights of the hotel chain's Tiki bars. To conceptualize the Tiki terminals, I began by scribbling a wild array of drawings (as shown in Figure 1.2).

The Tiki terminal incorporates a standard computer into its design. Starting with the idea that the Tiki should house (and hide) the computer itself, it is decided that a small form factor is required for the case and a flat LCD screen will be necessary for the display. Taking this into consideration, a flat-screen monitor will fit the bill perfectly. I will suggest to my client that they use an Apple iMac in the actual design, as the small domelike computer will easily fit into a Tiki base.

As the conceptual work proceeds from the 2D design stage, I begin to see the limitations of designing on a piece of paper. I soon realize that the next step is to start making small 3D models. Lacking the 3D computer design experience, I head out to the art supply store to pick up some air-dry clay and plasticine. Upon my return, I whip up a flurry of small Tiki terminal designs out of clay (as shown in Figure 1.3).

Figure 1.2: The Tiki terminal concept drawings

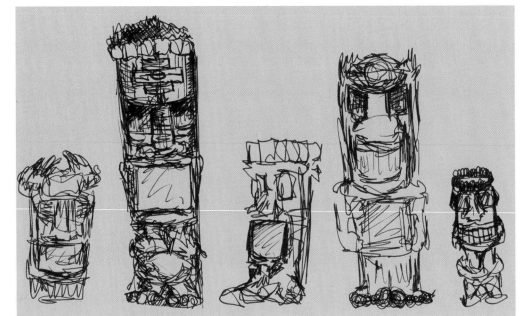

Figure 1.3: Early Tiki terminal clay models

I struggle with how to position the computer monitor. Most of the early designs show the display screen *inside* the Tiki's mouth. The design direction takes a change of course when I decide to have the Tiki *hold* the terminal in his hands instead. Most of my clay models follow this route. Finally, I unwrap a brand new 2 lb. block of plasticine and feverishly create the masterpiece shown in Figure 1.4.

When the plasticine mock-up is shown around, it becomes an instant hit. The bartender whips up an extra-special frozen concoction in the blender, and a mambo contest is held at lunchtime in the Tiki's honor. When my team returns from an extended lunch, they're hit with reality: now that there's a solid idea, how can they incorporate the Tiki terminal into the Tiki bar design that's taking shape in Photoshop?

Although the plasticine model is pretty cool, it's still a colorless six-inch-high hunk of clay. The team needs to place photo-realistic Tiki terminals into the Photoshop image, and they need the flexibility to try variations in color and texture to fit the decor. Inspiration strikes when I recall a segment about Maya on one of my favorite television shows, TechTV's *The Screen Savers*. A computer-generated model will allow the team all the flexibility they need to finish off the concept work.

Figure 1.4: The final Tiki terminal clay mock-up

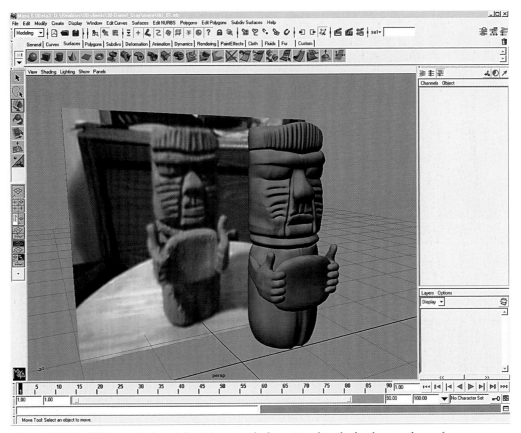

Figure 1.5: The Tiki terminal model in Maya, with the original in the background as reference

Lacking the expertise in 3D modeling and rendering, I decide to call in a Maya 3D pro. As there's no category for Maya 3D pros in the Yellow Pages (just yet), I phone a few friends in the know and soon find myself in contact with real-world Maya expert, Marc-André Guindon. After exchanging a few e-mails, I send a few digital photographs of the clay mock-up to Marc-André, who sets about creating a model of the Tiki terminal in Maya (as shown in Figure 1.5).

What took me days to create in actual clay, Marc-André was able to perfect with his stellar Maya skills in a few hours. Figure 1.6 shows a wireframe view of the Tiki terminal. Further, the Maya model is much easier to modify, whereas once my air-dried clay models hardened, I was out of luck. And while the plasticine model could be reworked, it only stood 6 inches high. I wasn't keen on spending a week (and a small fortune) building a life-size replica out of plasticine, nor would I have had the time or resources to build a physical scale model of the room to fit the Tiki. The process of mocking up projects like this in real life represents not only a significant investment in time, but in physical resources as well. Faux-finishing techniques take more effort in paint than they do in pixels. Materials can be imparted more readily in the virtual world, when compared with the real world. For instance, a gold texture can be applied in an instant with a shader, rather than in ages using the arcane technique of gold leaf.

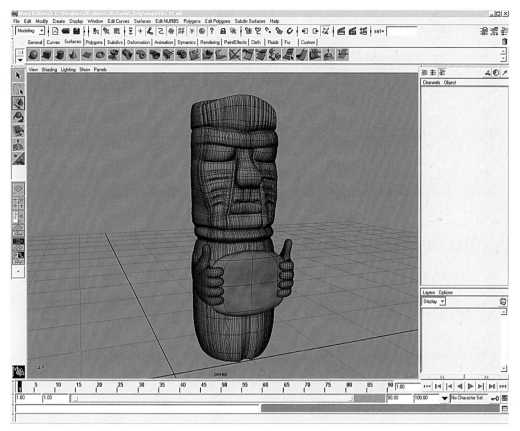

Figure 1.6: That's not a mystical tablet in the Tiki's hands; that's a flat-screen monitor!

Lighting and color are all important. Figure 1.7 shows the Tiki terminal in Maya, as Marc-André applies a screen shot to the Tiki's flat-screen monitor and begins the lighting work. As he's working on this stage, I'm rounding up a Tiki bar photograph from the kind folks at the Tiki Farm (see Figure 1.8). Although the Tiki bar photograph isn't of super-high resolution, it's close enough for us to continue with the mock-up work.

Once I have the Tiki bar photograph in hand, I send it to Marc-André, who promptly brings it into Maya to work on positioning. We decide to have two Tiki terminals to match the two barstools in the photograph. Each Tiki terminal is to be angled slightly outward, facing the barstools and following the boomerang shape of the bar. Figure 1.9 shows the scene in Maya, with the Tiki terminals perched on top of the bar. Different screen shots have been applied to each of the Tiki terminals, and the lighting is adjusted to jibe with the lighting in the Tiki bar photograph. Marc-André sends me the first test render (shown in Figure 1.10), and I'm absolutely ecstatic.

I'm blown away, seeing my crazy idea come to life in Maya. With deadlines tight, I promise not to ask for any changes other than a slight upward scaling of the Tiki terminals, to match the size of the bar and barstools. The next morning, Marc-André makes the tweaks, cranks out the final rendering, and puts it up on the FTP server.

Figure 1.7: The screen shot applied

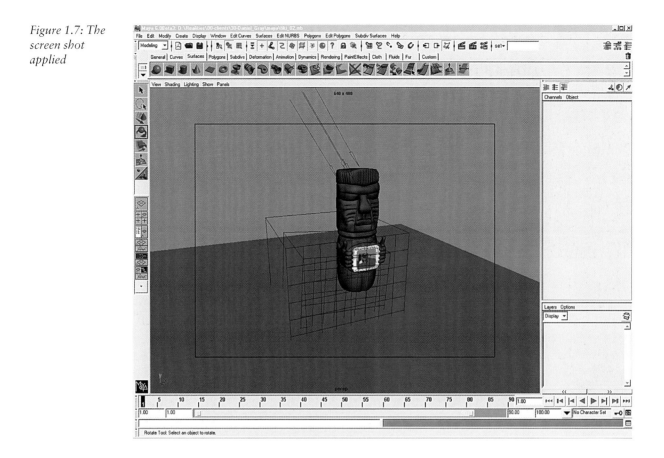

Figure 1.8: The Tiki Farm's fabulous Tiki bar

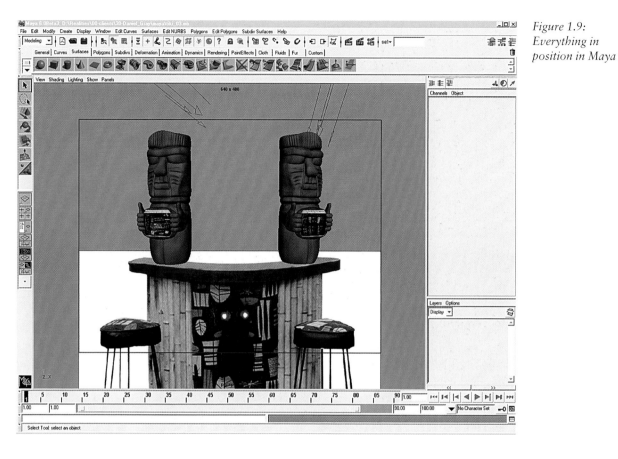

Figure 1.9: Everything in position in Maya

Figure 1.10: The first Tiki terminal test render

Figure 1.11: The final 2048-×-2048-pixel (2KB) Tiki terminal render

With the fabulous final 2KB render of the Tiki terminal models in hand, I bring the image into Photoshop and begin cranking out the Tiki bar composite image. I've determined that the fastest way to produce the image is to use three layers: the background, the Tiki bar, and the Tiki terminals. I purchase a number of suitable royalty-free stock photographs from istockphoto.com and settle on a pair of lovely tropical images, as shown in Figures 1.12 and 1.13.

I place the tropical scenes on layers in the composite Photoshop file, make a tight selection on the bar image, and copy and paste it into the image. There's a good bit of chunky fringe, so I set about softening that up with the Smudge tool. With the smudge work done, I jump into the final rendered image and make another tight selection, which I copy and paste into the composite. Marc-André kindly rendered shadows with the Tiki terminals, so I set about making them work with the bar surface. Once the muscle work is done, I finish up by applying a Film Grain filter (Grain 2, Highlight Area 3, Intensity 1). Within a short time, I've come up with a pair of suitable mock-ups for the marketing execs to marvel over, as shown in Figures 1.14 and 1.15. (Note the problematic fringe that surrounds the barstool legs.)

If my client wants more, I can build a patio floor in Maya and perhaps a small rock wall and some additional foliage behind the bar, to provide more perspective. As it is, the image is a bit rough, but certainly acceptable. With the comp of the Internet-equipped Tiki bar in hand, the design guns turn toward the next big element in the campaign, when the crew rolls back into the studio the next day.

Figure 1.12: *The palms are a bit large for scale in this shot, but we'll try it.*

Figure 1.13: *Nothing whispers tropical like a nice thatched roof.*

Figure 1.14: *A Photoshop rough of the Tiki terminals and bar*

Figure 1.15: Whoops, we forgot the keyboards!

Marc-André Guindon—Maya Expert

Marc-André Guindon (www.realities.ca) is a Maya expert extraordinaire. Aside from knocking out Tiki Terminals in his spare time, Marc-André has lent his talents to television shows, movies, and video games, as well as writing and editing books for Alias. Marc-André's television credits include work on *Xcalibur,* and his movie credits include special effects for the remake of *Dawn of the Dead,* as well as technical character direction for *Scooby Doo 2* (for Meteor Studios). He has also developed a lip-sync tool called *FatLips2* for Yulsoft.

Marc-André runs his own company, Realities, in Montreal, Canada.

Creating the EleMENTAL Woodie

The hotel chain isn't stopping with the Tiki terminals and bar. The marketing executives were so revved up with the Tiki terminal designs that they're ready to take the project over the top. Not only do they want to create a cool environment within the resorts, they want to create a special vehicle to promote and commemorate the launch of the Tiki bars.

And what better vehicle to launch a Tiki bar than an old-fashioned Woodie? But this isn't your grandfather's Woodie Wagon ... it's a chopped and channeled Honda Element! A Honda Element? We want it to be modern, and we want to make an already funky vehicle even more funky.

I decide that I need to take a Honda Element, cut the top down by six inches or so, slam it, and wrap the body in a fabulous wood veneer. This is much easier to do in Maya to show as a comp to the hotel execs, rather than going to the expense of having the custom shop crew do it from scratch (before the project is approved).

With an idea in mind, I set off to do some rough cuts in Photoshop to a stock Honda Element photo, snapped right from the dealer's lot. I begin by roughly silhouetting the top of the Element and knocking out the background shown in Figure 1.16. Then, I chop the top piece by piece—cutting, pasting, and repositioning each piece. Once the top is chopped and roughly touched up, it's time to flatten the image and move on to lowering the body. I select the entire body, carefully cutting around the wheel wells. Then, I cut, paste, and reposition the body, slamming it to the ground, as shown in Figure 1.17.

The Element's looking pretty cool, with its top chopped and its body lowered. The torch was taken to the roof pillars, and the springs were replaced in record time! Although this is a quick sketch, it's enough to get the dimensional flavor. With the bodywork in rough shape, it's not an appealing comp. Photoshop offers an easy answer to the design problem— a little tweaking with plug-ins and the chopped Element takes on an appearance somewhere between photo-realistic and watercolor marker (as shown in Figure 1.18).

As I'm having so much fun, I get a little carried away and do the chop job and water- color market treatment to an additional pair of photographs (see Figure 1.19). It's quick and dirty, sure, but it's cool.

The chopped Element rendering is looking pretty sweet. But I forgot to add the wood panels! A jump back to the rough chopped image in Photoshop allows me to experiment with wood veneers before reapplying the plug-ins to achieve the watercolor market effect, once again (as shown in Figure 1.20).

Figure 1.16: A stock Honda Element

Figure 1.17: The Honda Element—rough-chopped in Photoshop

Figure 1.18: The Honda Element—photorealistic marker effects in Photoshop

Figure 1.19: A bit less realism, a bit more watercolor

Figure 1.20: The Honda Element—first attempt at woody-ization

Once again, the design is a big hit in the office. After a busy morning, the crew sends a JPEG image to the hotel marketing folks, before heading off for another boisterous lunch filled with frivolity and frozen concoctions. Upon their return, the crew is overjoyed to hear that the marketing department loves the Element Woodie illustration. But there's a wrinkle. The client has asked to see the marvelous vehicle from different angles and in a number of different color schemes.

Here's where the Photoshop-only approach comes to a grinding halt. Multiple angles means that the cut-and-paste Photoshop work will have to be completed for each angle—and new photographs will have to be shot for each of these angles as well. Even worse, while the marketing department loves the watercolor marker renderings, they're asking for a more photographic treatment for the final presentation to senior management. Our clients don't quite have the imagination necessary to envision the finished vehicle. They want to see *exactly* what an Element Woodie might look like, not something that looks like a drawing but an actual photographic rendering.

It's time to call in the heavy artillery.

When you're working with clients, time is often a limiting factor. So, rather than re-take photos from all the different angles, the only way to do this project the right way is to create a chopped Honda Element Woodie in Maya. With some frantic Web searching and a handful of phone calls, I find Meshwerks, the only company in the entire world with an existing Honda Element model in Maya format. And even better, Meshwerks is willing to take on the digital customization work.

After a week's worth of work, Meshwerks produces an absolutely stunning photo-realistic rendering of the vehicle, which has been dubbed the EleMENTAL Woodie. The first image, as shown in Figure 1.21, is breathtakingly real. When the image is sent over to the hotel marketing staff, they're ecstatic.

You'll learn how Meshwerks created the stunning EleMENTAL Woodie in Chapter 10.

Figure 1.21: The EleMENTAL Woodie—final rendering

The Truth in Three Dimensions

As designers, we're often faced with dilemmas. Many of these problems have roots in our current capabilities and limitations. Although the examples presented here may seem a little far out, they're not all that far out of line. How many times has a client come to you with unreasonable expectations? How many times have you had to compromise your designs because of the impossible?

Although the previous examples sprang completely from my imagination, the solutions to the problems were found by hooking up with the right people. I did not have the 3D chops to complete these projects on my own, but I was wise enough to seek the assistance of highly skilled Maya artists that could turn my crazy dreams into reality. You'll meet Marc-André Guindon, the Maya artist who created the Tiki terminal model, in Chapter 8. And Meshwerks is covered in depth in Chapter 10, where you'll learn exactly how they took my marker drawings as inspiration for creating the photo-realistic EleMENTAL Woodie.

The Learning Curve

I would be remiss if I did not state the significance of the Maya learning curve. For many artists, the leap to 3D can be one of the biggest learning challenges of their careers—that is, after the mastery of the basic concepts of the arts. True mastery of Maya does not come in days, or weeks, or even months. It is not something that can be successfully approached on a casual basis. It takes a big commitment of time and, at times, a considerable test of will. But the positive results are inescapable: when you are capable with Maya, anything is possible.

Getting your head around Maya can be a challenge. I know that for a fact, as I've struggled with learning the program on my own, without the benefit of a classroom setting. However, as the popularity of 3D continues to grow, the learning resources do as well, and there are many online communities and Listservs of passionate Maya users who are always willing to lend a hand. Browsing through a local bookstore also turns up a wealth of books to help you learn Maya.

To fully enable the learning process, you must discard the constraints of working in two dimensions while retaining the knowledge you have of working with bitmap images and vector artwork. You'll still need to know how to push pixels and tweak Bèzier curves, but you'll need to learn how that applies to the third dimension.

Working in 3D isn't like working on a flat piece of paper. Rather, it's like working on a stage. Think of yourself as being in the business of designing theater sets, and you'll set the stage for success.

My breakthrough came while I was in the midst of envisioning the Tiki terminals. After creating pencil drawing after pencil drawing, I realized that I needed to create some clay models to fully work through the concept. That's when I bought the box of clay. I came home and immediately started whipping up Tiki designs, mostly horrid at first, but soon had my ideas gelling.

And this is what got me over the hump. Thinking in three dimensions isn't about having a computer for a brain. It's about looking at shape and form and the way that light bounces off surfaces. It's about creating something from nothing.

You can't expect to do well in 3D computer graphics if you do not grasp the basics of 3D design and modeling in the real world. I'm lucky in that I've always enjoyed working with clay, and yet it had been years since the last time I experimented in the medium (in a college 3D design class).

Other Options

If the demands of your craft leave little time for exploring Maya, you still have plenty of options. If ideas in your head need to be developed in 3D—but you lack the wherewithal to make it happen on your own—you can easily partner with a 3D artist. You'll see this in a number of cases in this book. A division of labor in a weighty design project that encompasses both 2D and 3D elements is a wise choice.

Two of the artists profiled in these pages—Michael Elins and Mirko Ilic—work in this manner. Both Michael and Mirko are producing high-end artwork that involves three-dimensional elements and are working in Photoshop, yet neither touches the controls in Maya. Instead, they team up with highly skilled Maya artists to produce artwork that smashes the barriers of conventional design.

Looking Forward

Once you understand the basics, it's not hard to build a case for the inclusion of 3D elements in your design work because 3D opens new worlds in so many ways. To fully grasp 3D, however, you must first open your mind to the possibilities. And you must acknowledge that while the rewards are many, there is a learning curve. Rest assured, there is no book that promises to teach you Maya in 24 hours (nor should there ever be). You can't learn Maya in a day, a weekend, or even a week. What's great is that you can get rolling and produce some cool stuff with some basics and some help from others. Because of the incredible depth of creative possibilities, you'll have to decide for yourself what level of Maya you might want to master. But that is beyond the scope of this book.

The intent of the next two chapters is to get you familiar with the Maya interface as you gain the basics of working in 3D. Although the next two chapters are a little more hands-on if you choose, the rest of the book serves an inspirational purpose, examining the studios and artists that are changing the way art gets made. By meeting the artists and learning how they create their artwork, you'll gain insight into the creative process and be inspired to craft your own masterpieces with Maya and Photoshop.

The Maya-Photoshop Connection

Dariush Derakhshani

If you've never used Maya, *let's get something straight: you won't learn Maya in a couple of chapters, and this book doesn't claim to teach you that. The best way to learn Maya is through experience and experimentation, just like any other software program— from Photoshop to your favorite word processor or MP3 player. This chapter aims to familiarize you with how these two worlds are different and, more important, how they interact and come together to work as a team toward a common goal, that of image creation. To start, we'll give you some background on how 2D and 3D differ and then some starter info to get you acquainted with Maya if you choose to download the Personal Learning Edition and start to experiment on your own in Chapter 3.*

Beyond 2D

Many of the skills you've already developed as a Photoshop user will serve you well in 3D work: painting, texturing, and lighting. By introducing the third axis, you can expand on those skills and, by extension, the images you create.

Fundamentally, using Maya involves a different way of thinking. That's not to say it's any more or less difficult or complicated than using Photoshop, just different. A painter who uses oils must change their technique when they decide they'd like to sculpt with sandstone. And they must change not just the actual method of sculpting, but how they approach the idea of creating changes. The process of interpreting the end goal becomes a different perception of image creation, and the better the artist understands how to begin that way of thought, the better equipped they will be when sitting down with the chisel and hammer.

When they are done with their sculpture, when they have indulged the way of the sculpture, they gain artistically, and even their future painting gains from the experience. It's similar in the world of digital content creation. It just depends on the tools you decide to use.

Learning Essential 3D Concepts

Working in 2D and 3D are radically different. The idea behind the method used to obtain an image using Photoshop is direct. Using Maya to achieve a similar image is a delicate balancing act, coordinating several fronts to the same end. In 2D image creation, it is important to know where you are in a linear progression from beginning to end. The image is started and painted or edited through a series of actions until it is suitable for the desired result.

In 3D image creation, however, you add a layer of complexity in the planning. For instance, a painting of car in Photoshop is complete when the car looks like you intended it to. In Maya, you may also need to consider a variety of possibilities. Will the back of the car be shown? Will the car doors need to be animated? Will the interior of the vehicle be shown? At any one time in Maya, you will need to know where you are in your scene and what each facet of your production needs.

2D Workflow versus 3D Workflow

Creating an image in 2D space in Photoshop involves *editing* existing pixels. Even if your canvas is bare, it is still a set frame of space with a set number of pixels in a canvas with a certain (though changeable) width and height upon which pixels are colored. Using brushes and other tools, you lay down colors to form the image.

Or perhaps you've acquired a scanned or digitized image that you are editing. Here the work mostly involves editing color ranges, cutting and pasting, moving parts of the image, and the like. It still boils down to editing existing pixels.

Creating an image in 3D space involves a wholly different philosophical approach. With Maya, you have an open space, bound by nothing. And the actual physical act of creating an image file from Maya is only the last part of the entire process of creating a scene, which typically begins with creating objects, or modeling. Because of this, you are not manipulating pixels as in Photoshop, but objects—most usually surfaces or models.

As such, Maya's workspace becomes a virtual space that you define from the *ground up*, specifying everything from the color to the lighting and cameras used to capture the image. As a matter of fact, you could say that Maya is arranging a physical scene with your own models, painting these objects to give them texture and color, lighting the scene, and taking its picture with a film camera.

Photoshop work is more akin to using paint strokes to fill your canvas or using photographic tools, a razor blade, and tape to manipulate what's on the print or photo. In this venue, the final image is already envisioned and is pursued directly by putting the colors where they need to be. With Maya, you work to define every element to come together in the end (through rendering) to *form* the final image in mind.

Furthermore, the actual tool sets in Maya and Photoshop are used differently. You can expect a more iterative process in 3D since it is not as direct an image creator as Photoshop. Photoshop's tools get to the point, and once you change something in an image, the chances it will affect and require changes to other parts of the image are slim. Working in Maya will show you that changes to one thing will more than likely affect many other things within the scene that may now need to be altered to stay harmonious in the scene; doing one thing in Maya will most likely require the adjustment and tuning of several *related* events. For instance, modeling an object is followed by texturing it (giving it color through a *shader*). Once the model is altered, the texture may also need to be altered to fit the new model. A change in a Photoshop image would be more direct and may not need tangential tinkering.

3D Workflow

The typical 3D workflow begins with creating the objects you want to manipulate. Although you can do this in a number of ways (such as 3D scanning), you almost always do so through the process of *modeling*. Using tools reminiscent of a sculptor's studio, you create and mold surfaces to make up the objects that populate your scene. You create curves, sweep spans, extrude parts of a shape, hammer, cut, and trim your way to a complete model or models.

This process typically calls for some idea of what you want in the scene even before you begin the work of creating it. Using reference materials from the Web, books, sketches, or even physical models will give you a great starting point.

Once you populate a scene, the next step in *CG* (computer graphics) creation is *texturing*. Objects in Maya are bare surfaces that are blank canvases. They have no surface properties except perhaps the most rudimentary color, gray by default. However, the act of texturing in Maya involves applying images, colors, or surface traits to your modeled surfaces to give you the ability to render them out looking right, with surface texture, with color, with highlights, and so on. Texturing and modeling can dance an intertwined waltz as you decide how you want your models to look.

Texturing is most commonly associated with Photoshop work because there is so much overlap. You can create textures and maps in Photoshop and import them into Maya to enhance the models and set the proper look for the scene. Also the workflow is quite similar, since you will be painting and applying attributes to make the images for texturing sing.

Once the textures are settled, you move on to *lighting*. This process involves setting up positions and intensities to illuminate your scene, much like the setup work of a photographer. After modeling, this is perhaps the next area of Maya that is intrinsically different from Photoshop. In Photoshop, you don't need to create illumination in your scene. You use the colors you paint or edit directly into your image to create the illusion of lighting. In Maya, you need to think as a photographer and decide how best to illuminate your scenes using Maya's lights. Fortunately, these lights are much like real lights, and you use many of the same methods you would use on a real set. Nonetheless, creating the illusion of light in an image is a much more indirect, though perhaps much higher fidelity, methodology.

The next step is optional and is the process of *animation*. Animation creates movement in your objects and your scene. Animation can be as simple as an object changing colors or the moving shadow of a sundial or as complex as a jogging human figure. Since most Photoshop work is on still images, animation is not an integral part of a Photoshop-Maya partnership, although this can be a lot of fun.

The final step in CG creation is *rendering*. Rendering is the technical process of converting all the vector data of your Maya scene into a viewable raster image such as a JPEG or a TIFF file. (See the "Vector versus Raster" section for more information.) But the process of rendering involves a bit more than the simple act of processing (through the computer would hardly consider it a simple act!). To get back to the photographer analogy, you shoot your Maya scene with a camera, whether still or moving.

A photographer needs to choose the correct camera, the proper film and exposure settings, and the right lenses. The lighting and composition done to this point lead up to *framing* the shot and shooting it to film. Rendering in Maya is much the same. You have to create a virtual camera and choose its settings to shoot your scene.

Here again, as in with lights, Maya cameras are analogous to real-life cameras. Consequently, a lot of the lingo in physical photography carries over into Maya work. You start by framing the shot. Here is where you will notice one of the great freedoms of 3D. You can place the camera almost anywhere you want to give you essentially unlimited angles from which to compose your scene. And it is also here that Photoshop and Maya are most similar and yet most different.

A good composition is a good composition no matter what. The ideas of basic design fall into place when you compose an image in Photoshop. In Maya, however, you consider these design ideals throughout the CG creation process, from modeling to rendering. It's just during the rendering phase that you finalize the position of your camera to frame the exact composition you want. With Photoshop, you begin with that composition in mind and work directly toward it by layering and placing images together. In Maya, once you model and arrange your scene, you can change your mind and alter the composition of the frame by merely moving the camera to gain a different angle and, perhaps, a completely different mood for your composition.

Once you set your framing and check all the aspects of your scene such as lighting and textures, you can click the Render button and watch it go. Well, you don't really watch it go; a watched render never boils. The computer takes over at this point and takes the scene as it has been defined and renders an image you can view or print.

Often, you don't finish with Maya; you perfect rendered images in other programs. Once you save an image to disk, you can use it as you wish. You can touch it up in an image editor such as Photoshop, or you can use a compositor such as After Effects to color-correct and mask animated sequences.

Contrast and Color

In Maya, you define color using textures as well as lights. In Photoshop, you paint color directly; in Maya, you define how objects behave to give you color. For example, you want to create a purple ball. In Photoshop, you simply paint a purple ball, complete with some bright highlights and areas of shadow. In Maya, you create a ball, define it as being purple through its shader, light it so the highlights and shadows fall where you want them, and render the ball. Furthermore, you can even create a blue ball and light it with red to give a purple result, but with a different feel altogether.

For example, to create a moody, contrasty image in Photoshop, you either paint it and/or use the brightness contrast filters as well as levels filters to change the coloring and contrast of the image (see Figure 2.1).

In Maya, you set up the scene with some bright lights that produce sharp highlights and dark shadows to make for a moody, contrasty scene (see Figure 2.2). Of course, you can

Figure 2.1: Using Photoshop, we adjusted the colors and contrast in this photo to create a sense of eerie mood.

process the rendered image(s) further in Photoshop using its filters and adjustments, but the initial mood of the image is typically obtained through the lighting and rendering and needs to be taken into account when you begin your scene.

Vector versus Raster

You've probably read about vector vs. raster a million times in other graphics books, but it's worth repeating this information here. Raster files are image files we use everyday. These files are defined on a pixel-by-pixel basis; they are a mosaic of colored pixels. And their image files are stored in the same way: Each pixel's color information from the top of the image to the bottom, from left to right, is defined by a series of values representing red, green, and blue values. This is why a high-resolution image makes for a large file size; the pixels are all accounted for in the file itself.

Vector files store image information through geometric algorithms and equations that *define* the image line by line, area by area, volume by volume. Each element of the image's design is stored as a geometric object or volume. The vector file is then rasterized to create an

Figure 2.2:
Using Maya,
we adjusted the
lighting in this
scene to produce
a misty look.

image that you can view on your screen. In other words, a vector file is rendered on the fly through your computer as it plays or is displayed. A Flash web animation is nothing more than a vector file that renders as you watch it on your PC. That's why a long Flash animation does not need a large file size. It is not defined pixel by pixel as a raster file is.

Software that produces 3D images stores information in vector format. This information is manipulated every time you work on the scene in Maya. When you render it, the scene is then translated into raster images that you see on your screen, defined pixel by pixel.

Figure 2.3: A raster image pixelates as it's scaled up.

Figure 2.4: A vector rendering of the same image displays smoothly as the vector scene is called up before it is rendered.

In Figure 2.3, the image on the left is viewed at 100% scale, but when it is blown up to four times that size, you will see *pixelation*. That is, you'll see jagged edges.

A vector image, however, always displays smoothly at any scaling factor, as shown in Figure 2.4.

2D Space versus 3D Space

This one's not so brainy; 2D and 3D spaces are actually quite similar. When working in Photoshop, width and height are defined in pixels, inches, or points that correspond to the size of the final product. You can easily change the size of your canvas at any time, but the size always relates directly to the size of the final image. This Photoshop canvas has a

Figure 2.5: In Photoshop, you create an image on the canvas.

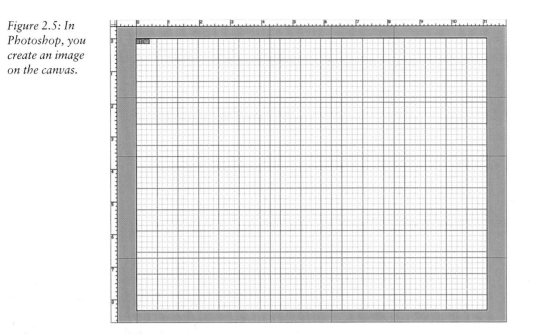

Figure 2.6: In Maya, you create your scene in 3D space, from which you render an image.

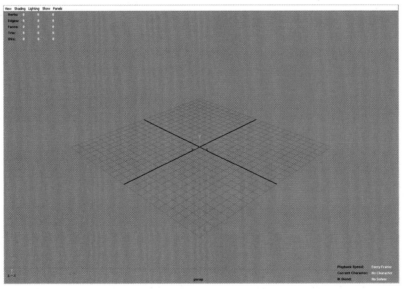

2D axis (see Figure 2.5). X is defined as the width from left to right, and Y is defined as the height from bottom to top. If the image is 800 pixels wide and 600 pixels tall, its coordinate space ranges from 0 to 800 in X and 0 to 600 in Y. Each pixel on the canvas has a coordinate that defines its location on that XY grid, with the *origin* of the image at (0,0), the pixel in the lower-left corner. The upper-right corner is defined as (800,600).

3D space is exactly the same, except that it has an addition axis for depth: Z. Therefore, 3D coordinate space is defined by an extra number, with its origin at (0,0,0). Objects in the 3D scene are defined in part by their location in the scene. Instead of a pixel having an XY position, a 3D object has an XYZ position. Now *where* that object ends up in your final rendered image depends on the view and angle you choose (see Figure 2.6).

Getting an image from that space involves defining a camera that snaps a shot from whatever angle you choose to best frame the 3D object(s). This turns everything in its view into a 2D frame with an XY resolution, just like a Photoshop file. To get your image, you basically say, "Give me an 800-×-600-pixel image of my 3D model from this angle."

Space and Composition

Since Maya is 3D, its workspace is different from that in Photoshop. With Photoshop, your canvas defines your compositional space right off the bat. In Maya, your camera ultimately defines this space but is free to capture any snapshot of your 3D workspace that you want. Therefore, the task of layout and composition is perhaps not the first task when you create an image. Of course, it is endlessly helpful to have a fantastic idea of where you want to go before you begin, but you have limitless potential to change your composition by either rearranging elements in the scene or by just rendering different cameras and views.

You can achieve different compositions of the same subject matter by merely moving the camera in Maya or even by changing its lens. Figure 2.7 shows a scene created in Maya, whose composition is easily changed. Doing so in Photoshop may be a far more involved task since the image must be recaptured, repainted, or recomposed from the beginning.

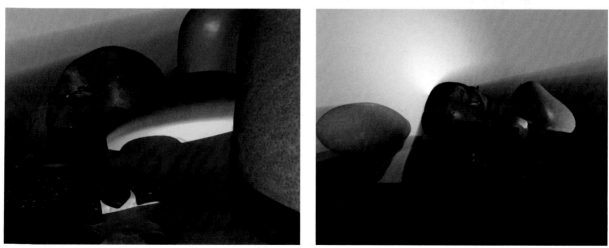

Figure 2.7: A Maya composition shown using different angles and filters

Title bar
Main menu bar
Status line
Shelf

Tool Box

Workspace

Time Slider
Range Slider
Command line

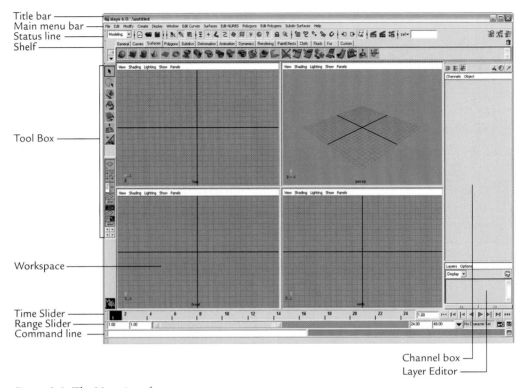

Channel box
Layer Editor

Figure 2.8: The Maya interface

Maya's Interface

Maya's interface (detailed above in Figure 2.8) is more intricate and involved than that of Photoshop. Its rich tool set is layered and boasts numerous functions and abilities that make it impossible to distill into the toolbar and palette approach of Photoshop. That's why it's important to understand a little bit about *how* the interface works in Maya.

Menu Bar

You will notice that, like all good programs, Maya has menus just below its title bar. Briefly, these menu choices depend on the tool set you need. By switching *menu sets*, as shown in Figure 2.9, you change your menu choices and tool access. The menu sets are organized according to function. For example, the Animation menu set gives you access to animation tools such as Set Key. Perhaps the Rendering menu set is the most associated with Photoshop work since it gives you access to texturing (or shading) and lighting functions.

Menu sets were created to keep all the functions of the program organized and easily accessible, much as the way in which filters are organized in Photoshop, according to function and sometimes according to the software maker.

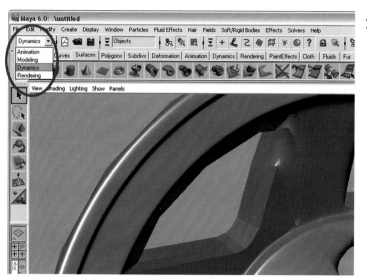

Figure 2.9:
The menu set

To change menu sets, select the menu you want from the drop-down menu in the upper-left corner immediately below the File menu. If you change menu sets, you'll notice that the first six menus remain constant, as does the last—Help.

Menu Set Hot Keys

To toggle between the menu sets, you can use the following hot keys:

F2	Animation	F4	Dynamics
F3	Modeling	F5	Rendering

Viewport Navigation

When Maya first loads, you will see a scene window labeled "persp" that has a grid in it and is surrounded by several icons, as shown in Figure 2.10. You use this scene window, known as a viewport, to view Maya's 3D world. Notice the View Axis icon in the lower-left corner of the viewport. This icon acts as a compass to indicate how you are oriented relative to the viewport. Each axis is color-coded:

- Red = X
- Green = Y
- Blue = Z

Think of the X and Y axes as your Photoshop canvas, but without borders. The canvas extends to infinity as opposed to a certain number of pixels defined in a Photoshop canvas. Now just add the Z axis to increase depth.

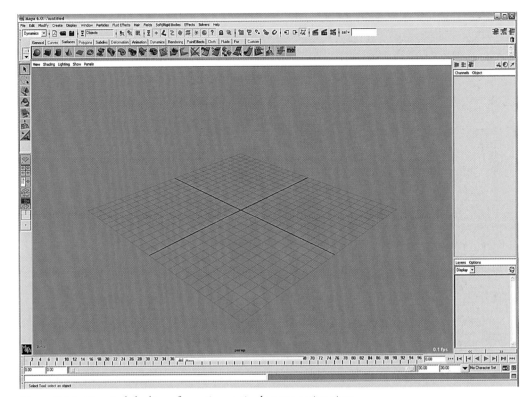

Figure 2.10: Maya's default configuration, a single perspective view

This perspective view is a camera view. Three other default views are available in all scenes. To view the other viewports, click in the perspective view to activate the view, highlighting its border, and press the spacebar. The Maya view is now subdivided into four views, as shown in Figure 2.11.

One of the viewports will be highlighted with a blue border, indicating that it is active. (The highlight color depends on the color scheme of your computer.) You can activate a viewport by clicking it with any mouse button, but it is recommended that you get in the habit of using the right mouse button to avoid deselecting your object(s). Even though four views are open, we are still dealing with only one document. In Photoshop, you can have as many documents open as your RAM can hold. In Maya, you can have only one document (scene) open at a time, though you could keep open multiple instances of Maya with different scenes. If you move the mouse over a viewport and press the spacebar again, the viewport the mouse was over will once again become a single enlarged view.

The "persp" viewport is the perspective view as seen through a camera. A *perspective* view shows depth. Objects farther away will seem smaller, and long lines in depth will taper to a vanishing point in the distance. The other three views (side, front, top) are *orthographic* views; that is, they are straight-on views that do not distort in perspective. The scale of objects is not altered by their distance to the camera, so sizing up objects and comparing them is best done in the orthogonal views.

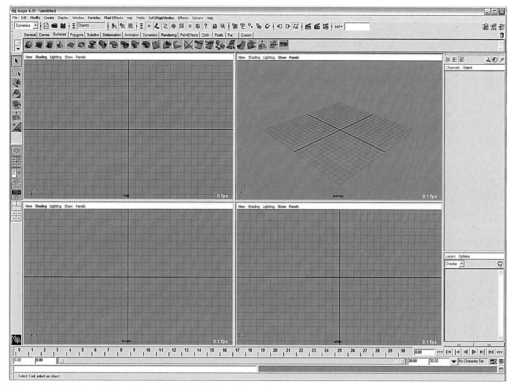

Figure 2.11: Maya's interface subdivided into four viewports

Maya has many controls for navigating its viewports or panels using a three-button mouse and keyboard combinations.

To familiarize yourself with the Maya interface, open the Shapes.ma file on the CD that came with this book. Choose File → Open Scene.

The scene opens in a single perspective view, with a blue cone, a green cube, and a red sphere in the distance. Like Photoshop, Maya has many built-in keyboard shortcuts, called hot keys. Pressing the F key, for Frame Selection, zooms you in close enough to get a good look at objects. In Maya, if nothing is selected and you press F, Maya frames all the objects in your scene within the currently active viewport.

And here we see the powerful advantage of 3D: the ability to view an object from *any* angle, and the ability to move among the objects (Figure 2.12). To change your point of view, hold down the Alt key (Mac users, hold down the Option key instead) and drag around the viewport with the left mouse button. To pan the view around, hold down the Alt key (Option for Mac) and drag with the middle mouse button. To zoom in and out on objects, hold down the Alt key (Option key for Mac) and drag with the right mouse button. Notice how the View Axis icon changes with your point of view within the perspective viewport.

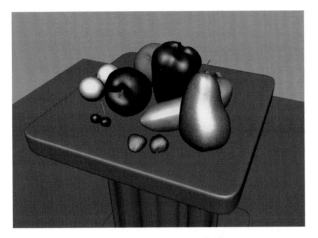

Figure 2.12: In 3D space, you can view your subject matter from virtually any angle.

Press the spacebar to display the four-view layout we were looking at earlier, and try the mouse movements in the nonperspective (orthogonal) viewports. Notice that rotating only works in the perspective viewport; there is no sense of depth in the orthographic views.

In our **Shapes.ma** scene, you may have noticed that the orthographic viewports are drawing the objects as wireframes. If you want Maya to draw the objects within a viewport as solids like you see in the perspective view of this scene, hold the mouse over the viewport and press 5. To return to a wireframe view, hold the mouse over the viewport and press 4.

The Tool Box

Just as Photoshop has a Tool window, Maya has a Tool Box, shown in Figure 2.13 and further detailed in Table 2.1, that contains the tools you use most often when working in a Maya scene.

You use these tools to manipulate the objects in your scene: Select Tool, Lasso Tool, Move (a.k.a., Translate) Tool, Rotate Tool, Scale Tool, Soft Modification Tool, and Show Manipulator Tool.

At the bottom of the Tool Box are several screen layouts that let you change the interface with a single click. Different work in Maya may call for different layouts of the viewports and panels. If you were doing a lot of texturing, you might want one large window side by side with a panel window of the Hypershade (where you access shaders and textures). Try different layouts by clicking any of the preset icons in the Tool Box.

The Shelf and Status Line

Running across the top of the screen are two rows of tool icons. The top row, sporting smaller icons, is called the *Status line* (shown in Figure 2.14) and contains functions for selecting objects and object components called Selection Modes and Selection Masks. Since objects can be manipulated on a component scale, meaning you can shape an object by moving points, or *vertices*, on the surface, using Selection Modes and Masks is much easier and faster. It's like

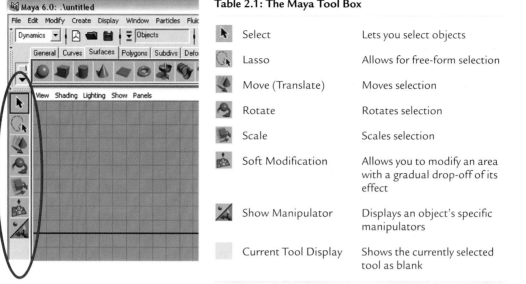

Figure 2.13: The Tool Box

Table 2.1: The Maya Tool Box

	Select	Lets you select objects
	Lasso	Allows for free-form selection
	Move (Translate)	Moves selection
	Rotate	Rotates selection
	Scale	Scales selection
	Soft Modification	Allows you to modify an area with a gradual drop-off of its effect
	Show Manipulator	Displays an object's specific manipulators
	Current Tool Display	Shows the currently selected tool as blank

Figure 2.14: The Status line

Figure 2.15: The shelf

being able to switch from a micro to a macro scale. You'll become familiar with these icons as soon as you begin creating in Maya. For a quick peek, though, you can roll over the icons with your mouse pointer to display the tool's name. As a matter of fact, that is true of all icons in Maya; you can see a tool's name by moving your mouse pointer over its icon or button. It's a great way to get familiar with the Maya UI.

Below the Status line is a row of tabbed *shelves*. These shelves, grouped according to tool function, give you easy access to a wide range of Maya tools and functions, from modeling and surfacing options to rendering and lighting tools. The Shelf (see Figure 2.15) is fully customizable, so you can add your own tools in the order of your preference.

You can also use hot keys to toggle between the tools. Use W for the Move tool, E for the Rotate tool, R for the Scale tool, or Q to deselect any translation tool (which will hide its manipulator) and revert to the Select tool.

select the objects in the proper order. This actually helps you figure out commands and tool sets for almost all tools. If you're unsure where to go or click next, check here before calling your mom.

Maya Geometry

Even if you're not going to be creating your own models in Maya, it's good to have some basic knowledge of how Maya's modeling tools work. If you are up for doing your own modeling, you'll want to get the basics down first by reading other books such as *Introducing Maya 6: 3D for Beginners*.

Maya works by defining a scene full of objects, from the models themselves (*geometry*) to lights, textures, and shaders. These objects form the image once the scene is rendered. Geometry is formed with surfaces that are usually either created with curves (geometric lines) or from primitive objects. *Primitives* are basic shapes and volumes in Maya that are used as bases from which to model things. Maya has three kinds of geometry:

Polygons (polys) *Faces* make up poly surfaces. Faces are the flat surface areas where three or more points are connected. These points are called *vertices*. The contact border in between each face is called an *edge*. Figure 2.20 shows a poly sphere. Notice how the faces form the surface. In Maya, you can edit each of the component levels (vertex, edge, face), so you can effectively model your surface. Moving a component such as a vertex directly alters the surface. Polys have great control over shape, and most poly models comprise of hundreds or thousands of faces—all connected together as a single surface. However, poly surfaces tend to be jagged or faceted and not perfectly smooth unless you use extraordinary numbers of faces.

NURBS Curves called *isoparms* (reminiscent of Photoshop's paths) make up NURBS surfaces. These surfaces are based on Non-Uniform Rational B-Splines. Figure 2.21 shows a NURBS sphere and its components. NURBS are calculated differently than polygons. With polygons, since the vertices are directly on the faces and hence the surface, there is a direct correlation in editing: when you move a vertex, the edge and face

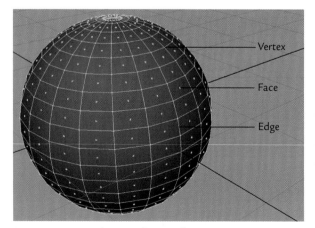

Figure 2.20: A polygon sphere and its components

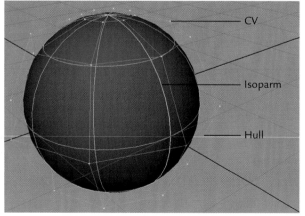

Figure 2.21: A NURBS sphere and its Components

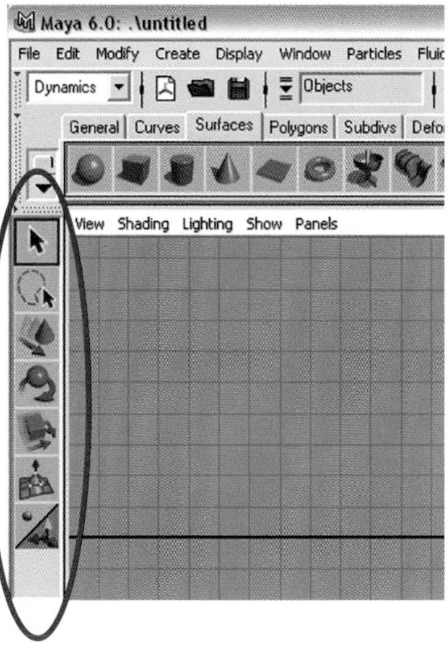

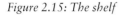

Figure 2.13: The Tool Box

Table 2.1: The Maya Tool Box

▶	Select	Lets you select objects
	Lasso	Allows for free-form selection
	Move (Translate)	Moves selection
	Rotate	Rotates selection
	Scale	Scales selection
	Soft Modification	Allows you to modify an area with a gradual drop-off of its effect
	Show Manipulator	Displays an object's specific manipulators
	Current Tool Display	Shows the currently selected tool as blank

Figure 2.14: The Status line

Figure 2.15: The shelf

being able to switch from a micro to a macro scale. You'll become familiar with these icons as soon as you begin creating in Maya. For a quick peek, though, you can roll over the icons with your mouse pointer to display the tool's name. As a matter of fact, that is true of all icons in Maya; you can see a tool's name by moving your mouse pointer over its icon or button. It's a great way to get familiar with the Maya UI.

Below the Status line is a row of tabbed *shelves*. These shelves, grouped according to tool function, give you easy access to a wide range of Maya tools and functions, from modeling and surfacing options to rendering and lighting tools. The Shelf (see Figure 2.15) is fully customizable, so you can add your own tools in the order of your preference.

You can also use hot keys to toggle between the tools. Use W for the Move tool, E for the Rotate tool, R for the Scale tool, or Q to deselect any translation tool (which will hide its manipulator) and revert to the Select tool.

The Channel Box

To the right of the screen, running from top to bottom, is the *Channel box*, which contains almost all the pertinent information you need about objects in your scene. The Channel box (see Figure 2.16) gives information about objects' position, scale, rotation, and so forth, but also provides an alternate option for interacting with objects. When you select a movable object, the top portion of the Channel box displays the name of the object and information about its position, rotation, and scale settings.

The Layer Editor

The Layer Editor (see Figure 2.17) is just beneath the Channel box and serves a similar purpose to the Layers Window in Photoshop. Along with controlling visibility, the Layer Editor in Maya controls how the object will be drawn and whether the object can be selected. Unlike Photoshop's Layers Window, the order in which the layers appear in the Layer Editor have nothing to do with whether object A is drawn in front of or behind object B. The renderer does that automatically according to the position of the objects in the scene in relation to the camera. You can place more than one object on a single layer in Maya—hundreds, if you want.

Creating layers in Maya is as easy as creating layers in Photoshop and serves a similar purpose—to organize your work. To create your own layer, simply choose Layers → Create Layer from the Layer Editor's menu. A new layer appears beneath the others. To customize

Figure 2.16:
The Channel box

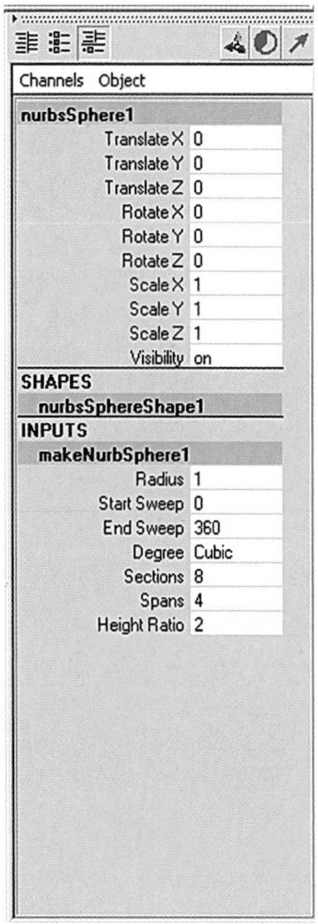

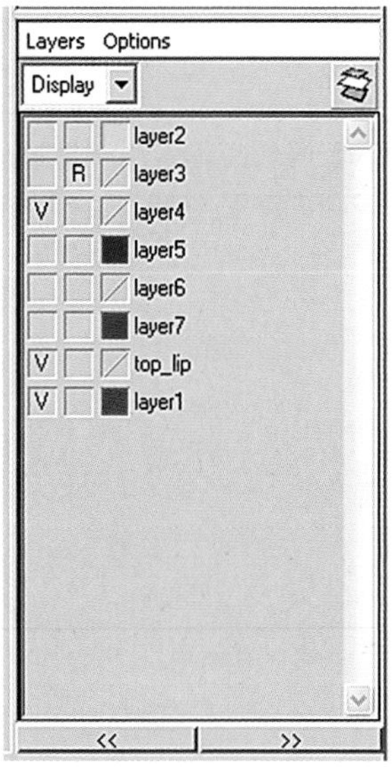

Figure 2.17:
The Layer Editor

a new layer, double-click its entry in the Layer Editor to open the Edit Layer dialog box (see Figure 2.18). Type a name in the Name field. What you choose from the Display Type drop-down list affects the appearance and selectability of any objects you place in the layer, though this is markedly different from Photoshop display layers and transform modes. Display modes in Maya are a further help in organization and don't necessarily change the outcome of the render, as would making a layer a Screen Transfer mode in Photoshop, for example. These display modes help you navigate the many objects in a scene by turning some on or off or making some selectable and some not.

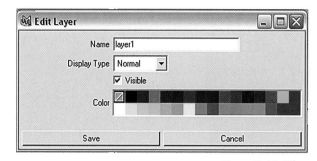

Figure 2.18: The Edit Layer dialog box

These toggles change how your Maya object is displayed in the viewports:

Normal Objects appear normally in your viewports and can be selected.

Template Objects are in a nonselectable gray wireframe, even if in shaded view.

Reference Objects display normally in shaded mode but cannot be selected.

The color swatch indicates the color of an object in wireframe mode when the display type is set to Normal in the Edit Layer dialog box. By changing the color of a layer, you are not changing the color of the object when it is rendered, only it's viewport display for organization. The Visibility check box determines whether objects in that layer are visible.

Clicking in the first of the three boxes next to the layer name in the Layer Editor below the Channel Box, toggles visibility, and clicking in the second box cycles through the display options for that layer. Renaming layers is as simple as in Photoshop; simply double-click the layer name and type the new name. To put objects in layers, select the objects, right-click the layer name, and choose Add Selected Objects from the context menu.

Time Sliders/Playback Controls/Help Line

Running across the bottom are sliders that set the time or frame range of your animation. To the right of these sliders are VCR-like controls to play the animation in your scene for previews. These will more than likely not be much of a factor in creating most still-image Photoshop work. The Help line (see Figure 2.19), the text line at the very bottom of the screen, gives you information about the currently active tool.

Let's say for example that you are using a surfacing tool that requires you to select objects in a certain order to create the desired surface. The Help line will prompt you to

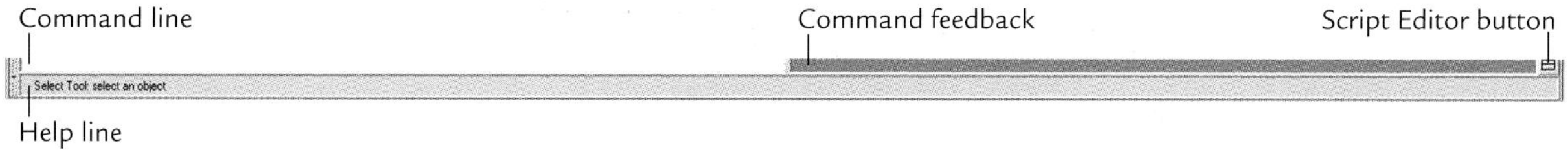

Command line   Command feedback   Script Editor button

Select Tool: select an object

Help line

Figure 2.19: The Help Line gives you valuable feedback and prompts.

select the objects in the proper order. This actually helps you figure out commands and tool sets for almost all tools. If you're unsure where to go or click next, check here before calling your mom.

Maya Geometry

Even if you're not going to be creating your own models in Maya, it's good to have some basic knowledge of how Maya's modeling tools work. If you are up for doing your own modeling, you'll want to get the basics down first by reading other books such as *Introducing Maya 6: 3D for Beginners*.

Maya works by defining a scene full of objects, from the models themselves (*geometry*) to lights, textures, and shaders. These objects form the image once the scene is rendered. Geometry is formed with surfaces that are usually either created with curves (geometric lines) or from primitive objects. *Primitives* are basic shapes and volumes in Maya that are used as bases from which to model things. Maya has three kinds of geometry:

Polygons (polys) *Faces* make up poly surfaces. Faces are the flat surface areas where three or more points are connected. These points are called *vertices*. The contact border in between each face is called an *edge*. Figure 2.20 shows a poly sphere. Notice how the faces form the surface. In Maya, you can edit each of the component levels (vertex, edge, face), so you can effectively model your surface. Moving a component such as a vertex directly alters the surface. Polys have great control over shape, and most poly models comprise of hundreds or thousands of faces—all connected together as a single surface. However, poly surfaces tend to be jagged or faceted and not perfectly smooth unless you use extraordinary numbers of faces.

NURBS Curves called *isoparms* (reminiscent of Photoshop's paths) make up NURBS surfaces. These surfaces are based on Non-Uniform Rational B-Splines. Figure 2.21 shows a NURBS sphere and its components. NURBS are calculated differently than polygons. With polygons, since the vertices are directly on the faces and hence the surface, there is a direct correlation in editing: when you move a vertex, the edge and face

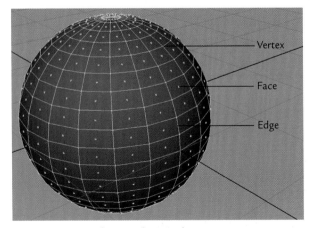

Figure 2.20: A polygon sphere and its components

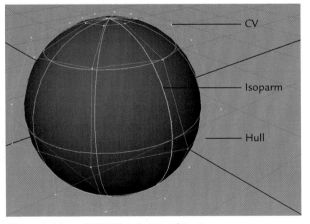

Figure 2.21: A NURBS sphere and its Components

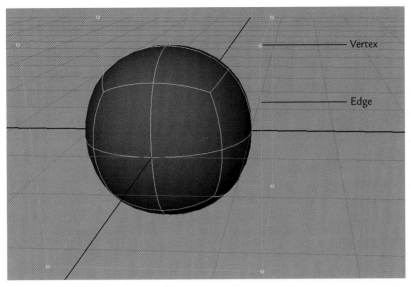

Figure 2.22: A SubD sphere and its components

adjust with it. NURBS are surfaces that always attempt to stay as smooth as possible. To that end, a NURBS surface has fewer points (called control vertices, or CVs) than a poly's vertices, and the resulting surface stretches from these CVs in a smooth manner.

NURBS are especially good for organic models. NURBS modeling, however, uses several patches to form a complex surface.

Subdivision Surfaces (SubDs) The same kind of vertices and edges that make up polys also make-up subdivision surfaces. But this style of modeling goes a step further to use the best features of polys and NURBS. The editing points (called vertices) are directly on the surface, as with polys, and are easy to edit. However, SubDs also have a layer of control that closely resembles how NURBS works so that SubDs are smooth like NURBS, but are simple single surfaces like polys. The resulting surface of a SubD edits much like a NURBS surface, giving you smoothness, by allowing you to control which areas of the surface have a large number of faces. Plus, you can switch between more or less detailed modes of editing a SubD surface, which increases or decreases the number of vertices you have to edit as needed.

Curves

Maya curves work much like Photoshop paths, with some important differences. Whereas Maya curves are used to generate surfaces (usually NURBS, but you can create polys as well), the curves themselves are never drawn, meaning they do not render, as opposed to curves drawn and seen in Photoshop images. The curves in both programs are based on the same equations—they both use Bèzier math—and curves in Maya are edited only slightly differently than they are in Photoshop, by manipulating the curve's CVs, as shown in Figure 2.23. Moving these points changes the shape of the curve, similar to altering Photoshop paths using the Pen tool, though Maya does not give you tangent handles as Photoshop path points do. Naturally, curves in Maya also have the added benefit of being three dimensional.

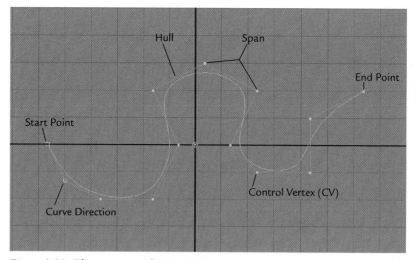

Figure 2.23: The anatomy of a NURBS curve

Like the geometry we've already seen in Maya, curves are made up of components as well. These components control the shape of the curve and can be used for editing, as with surfaces and their components.

Maya and Photoshop Interaction

The greatest point of interaction between Photoshop (or any image-editing program) and Maya is during texturing. As you texture a model, you go back and forth between Maya and your image editor a number of times to get placements, colors, and so forth just right. However, new to Maya 6 is the ability to read Photoshop files directly and to handle multiple layers within those Photoshop files.

Just like a Photoshop canvas has x and y coordinates to pinpoint pixels, surfaces in Maya have coordinates measured with u and v that pinpoint location. Matching the areas of an image to a particular area of a surface can take some doing. But when you're able to export a template (called a UV Snapshot) within a Photoshop layer, you're halfway there. Also Maya 6 lets you assign different layer folders within a Photoshop file to specific attributes of a shader for ultimate control, without having to generate several image files to assign to each shader attribute separately.

In short, a shader in Maya has several features defined by attributes, such as Color, Transparency, Bump, and so on, that ultimately define how the surface renders and looks. Previously, you had to generate more than one image file and then individually assign these shader attributes to map the textures to make your object look the way you want. For example, if you were texturing a simple window pane, you would want an image map that would make the areas of glass in the window transparent. The edges of the window (the pane) will remain opaque however and have a color map to make the window frame wood colored. This required generating two images that essentially lined up with each other that could be assigned to Color and Transparency of your window shader.

In Maya 6, you can create one PSD file and make a separate black-and-white image layer to define transparency that defines the glass area, while painting on another layer the wood color for the frame. This cuts down workflow and makes it easier to line things up in Photoshop to import into Maya.

We will explore texturing concepts with Maya and Photoshop in more detail and with hands-on practice in the next chapter.

Next Step

No doubt, as your original experiences with Photoshop will attest, gaining a working knowledge of graphics software takes time and practice. The more you play with Maya's interface and tool sets, the more you will learn. Although using Maya is a different way of thinking than using Photoshop, the purpose is the same: making great images. Now that you have some knowledge of how things work in Photoshop and Maya and how to get around in Maya, you're ready to merge the two worlds and get a taste of how you can put your Photoshop skills to use while working in Maya. In the next chapter we will create a few textures to add into a prebuilt Maya scene to better understand how these two programs can work together.

three

Introduction to Maya: Texturing with Photoshop

Dariush Derakhshani

Now that you have some insight into how Maya and Photoshop work together and how they work differently, we can dive into a couple of quick exercises to get you familiar with how an artist can use both programs hand in hand to create images.

Mapping Exercise: Simple Image Maps

We're starting with a simple NURBS model of a wine bottle that we need to shade to look like a real wine bottle, and then we'll use Photoshop to add a couple of labels to it. This exercise will cover basic shading and texturing techniques using Maya 6 to work with Photoshop PSD files directly.

The Three-Button Mouse

Whether you're using Maya on a PC or a Mac, you'll need a three-button mouse. If you have only a two-button mouse, you can most likely use the wheel as the third button. With Maya 6, you can also use the mouse wheel to zoom into or out of a view panel.

The exercises in this chapter assume you are using a three-button mouse. The left mouse button (LMB) acts as the primary selection button, the right button (RMB) activates several shortcut menus, and the middle mouse button (MMB) lets you move within the Maya interface and move objects themselves.

The Model: A Wine Bottle

Copy the Wine_Bottle project from the book's CD to your hard disk. Load the scene `Bottle_Texture_v01.mb`.

The wine bottle is a simple revolved surface from an outline curve. You can certainly make your own bottle to use, but to follow along better, using the supplied model (see Figure 3.1) to begin with is a better idea.

We created the bottle's surface using the Revolve tool in Maya. It is revolved from a curve that loops back on the inside of the bottle, to give the glass some thickness. This approach plays an important part in lighting and rendering the bottle since glass has a thickness. The bottle has a gray label around it already, though no image has been applied to it.

Overall Shading

To get an idea of how shaders work in Maya, and what their attributes mean, we'll start by giving the bottle a simple glass texture before we move on to applying images to the label. Most wine bottles are a deep forest green and are see-through to a good extent. We'll start by opening the Hypershade window (choose **Window → Rendering Editors → Hypershade**) to access the scene's shaders. You edit most shaders in the Hypershade window, which is shown in Figure 3.2.

The Hypershade Window

The Hypershade window displays the shaders and textures in your scene in the upper half. You use the bottom half, called the *work area*, to manipulate shaders and interconnect them. Maya's inner

Figure 3.1: The wine bottle

workings are based on how objects interrelate. When you attach an image, such as a wine label, for example, you are connecting the image's color into the shaders *color* input. By doing this, you can render out this image as the color of whatever object(s) are textured with that shader.

By using a graphical flowchart layout, you can quickly see how shader nodes connect. When several shading and texturing nodes are connected, you have created a *shading network*. More on this soon. The Hypershade's three main areas are: the *create panel* on the left; the *render node display* on the top, which shows you the existing shaders in the scene; and the *work area*, where you can adjust shader networks.

The Create Panel

In the Create panel, you can create any shader and its supporting textures by simply selecting its icon. Shaders are organized into sections according to their type of node. When you click to create a node, it appears in the top and bottom parts of the Hypershade.

The Render Node Display

Clicking a shader's icon selects that node in Maya, and double-clicking the icon opens the Attribute Editor for that node. To work with the shader network, you can MMB drag

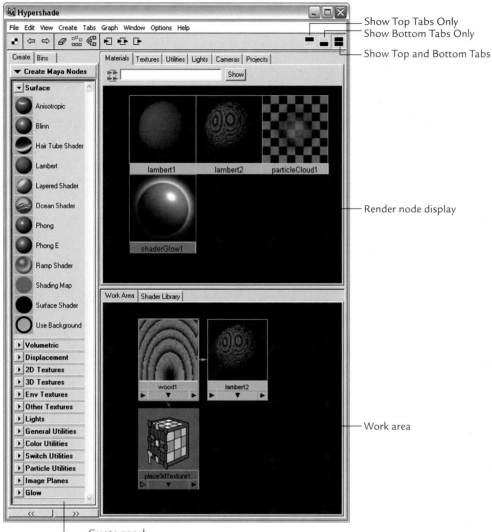

Figure 3.2: The Hypershade window

the icon into the work area below to access the connections between nodes. Navigating in the Hypershade is similar to navigating the viewport windows; you use the Alt key and mouse controls.

The Work Area

The work area is a workspace where you connect nodes to create texturing effects, such as attaching an image file to a bump map of a shader to give its object a tactile quality when it renders. You will see how this works later in this chapter.

Back to the Bottle

Meanwhile, back in the viewport, the bottle is still gray. We will create a simple green glass shader to assign to the bottle.

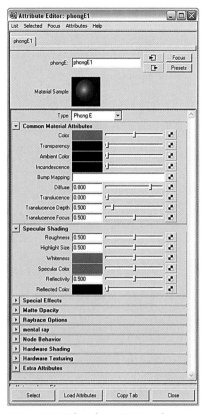

Figure 3.3: The phongE1 Attribute Editor

1. Create a Phong E shader by clicking its icon in the Create Maya Nodes panel. Double-click the phongE1 icon that appears in the Hypershade to open the Attribute Editor, which is shown in Figure 3.3.

   The attributes in this window affect how the shader looks when the scene is rendered. The primary attributes are **Color**, **Transparency**, **Incandescence**, and **Bump Mapping**.

2. To make the bottle green, click the gray swatch next to **Color** to open the Color Chooser window.

The Color Chooser window (Figure 3.4) is similar to Photoshop's Color Picker window, and they both work remarkably similarly. Figure 3.5 shows Photoshop's Color Picker window.

In the Maya Color Chooser window, set the color to a deep green with an HSV of about (99, 0.70, 0.16). HSV stands for Hue Saturation and Value, and is one of the ways you can define color in a digital image. Since the V number is low, its value will be low, making the color a very dark green. That will be fine here.

3. For transparency, we'll start simply. Bring down the transparency slider to about one-third lighter

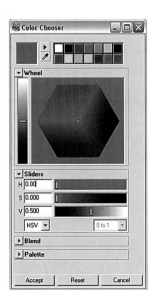

Figure 3.4: The Color Chooser window

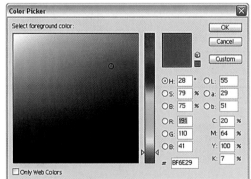

Figure 3.5: Photoshop's Color Picker window

than black. If you click the swatch to open the Color Chooser window, the V value of the HSV for the gray should be about 0.385.

4. Name the material *Glass* by changing the name phongE1 at the top of the Attribute Editor window. MMB drag the Glass shader onto the bottle to assign the Glass shader to the bottle. You can also select the bottle in the viewport, RMB click the Glass shader in the Hypershade window, and select Assign Material to Selection from the marking menu. Your bottle should look like that in Figure 3.6.

5. To check your shaders, you should render them every now and then; so let's quickly set up the render settings. Open the Render Globals window by choosing **Window** → **Rendering Editors** → **Render Globals** (see Figure 3.7). Set the resolution to 640 × 480 under the Common tab, and set Anti-Aliasing Quality to Intermediate Quality Preset under the Maya Software tab, as shown in Figure 3.7. This will give you a good-looking render without the time needed for a very high quality render such as the Production Quality Preset. Click the Render icon (shown here at right) in the Status Line to see a test of your bottle. Maya automatically uses a simple default lighting setup to light your scene.

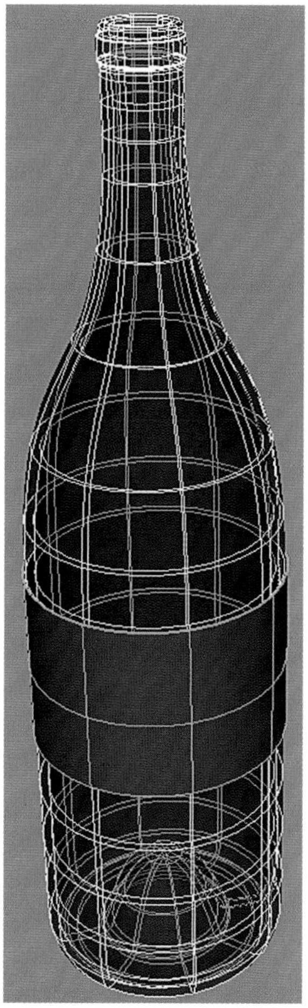

Figure 3.6: The wine bottle with the Glass shader applied

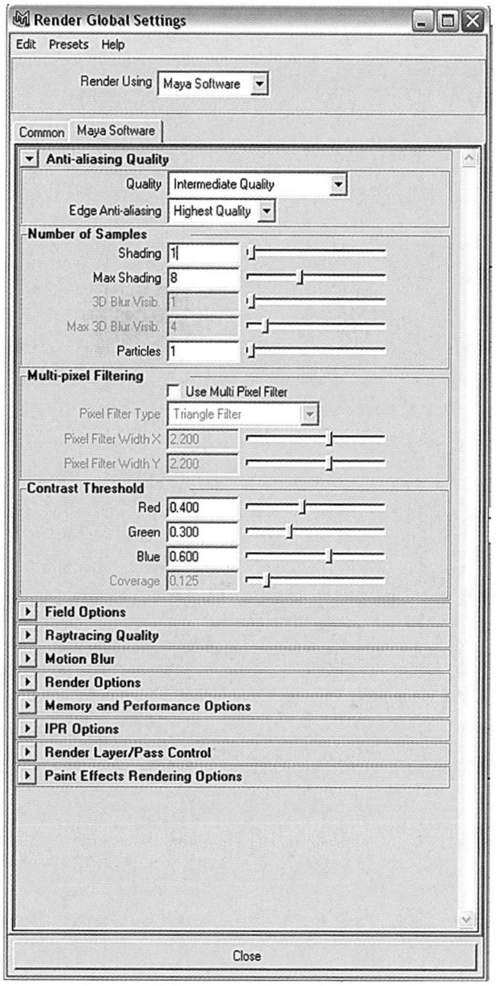

Figure 3.7: The Render Globals Window

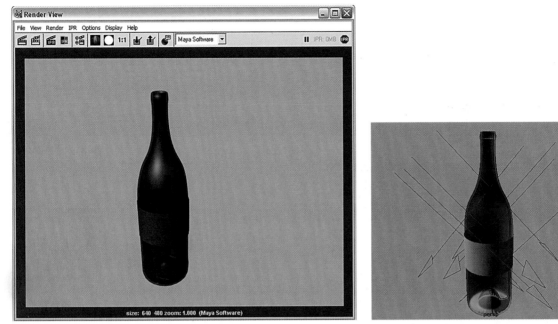

Figure 3.8: A test render of the wine bottle with a gray background

Figure 3.9: Orient the lights to illuminate both sides of the bottle

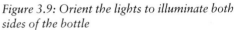

6. Now, let's make more than just a black background. In the persp view panel, choose **View** → **Camera Attribute Editor**. In the Environment section, set Background Color to a medium gray. This will show off the bottle better than a black background, as shown in Figure 3.8.

7. We'll also need a light other than the default light Maya uses in the absence of any other lights. Choose **Create** → **Lights** → **Directional Light**. The light appears at the origin pointing back. Rotate it to light the left side of the bottle. Create another directional light to illuminate the right side of the bottle, as shown in Figure 3.9. You can scale the lights up to make them more accessible in the viewport to orient them properly. That will *not* affect the lights' brightness or other attributes, just the size.

8. The first light creates a highlight to travel down the edge of the bottle. Set that light's intensity level to 2.5, and leave the second light's **intensity** at 1. The intensity value controls the amount of emitted light emitted. The higher the number, the brighter the light.

The Wine Label

So far, we've played with Maya shaders to make the bottle into glass, and we inserted a couple of lights to illuminate the bottle better, as shown in Figure 3.10. Now, we'll concentrate on attaching a label. The scene file **Bottle_Texture_v02.mb** in the Wine_Bottle project will catch you up to this point by giving you a bottle that is already shaded and lighted for you.

Figure 3.10: A test render of the bottle with the new lights   *Figure 3.11: The Create Render Node window*

To assign a simple image map to the label, follow these steps.

1. Open the Hypershade, create a Lambert shader by clicking its icon in the left side panel, and double click its icon once it's created on the right to open the Attribute Editor. Click the checkered map button (shown here at right) to map a texture on the **Color** attribute of the new Lambert shader. This opens the Create Render Node window, as shown in Figure 3.11.

2. Select the file node, and make sure the radial buttons at the top of the window are set to Normal. The Attribute Editor now displays the attribute for the file node. Next to the **Image Name** attribute, click the folder icon to open the File Browser. Find the wine_label.tif file in the sourceimages folder of the Wine_Bottle project. If your project is set to Wine_Bottle on your hard drive as it should to be, the File Browser should open at the sourceimages folder. Double-click the file to load it. Figure 3.12 shows the Attribute Editor window with the image file loaded.

3. To assign the label's new shader to the label geometry, select the label in a Maya viewport, RMB click the new Lambert shader you created, and select Assign Material to Selection. Test render it out, and you should have the result shown in Figure 3.13. The label is off-axis; it is rotated the wrong way.

You can fix the improperly mapped label in two ways. You can either rotate the image 90 degrees in Photoshop and resave the file, or you can use Maya's texture placement node to reposition the label. We'll try that since it's the fastest and most interactive solution.

Figure 3.12: The file node

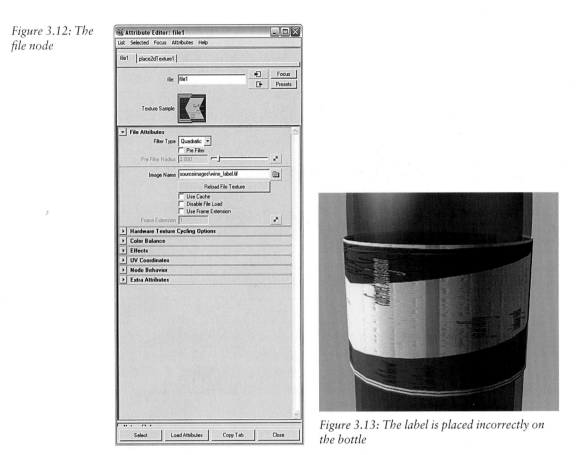

Figure 3.13: The label is placed incorrectly on the bottle

4. To orient the label properly, in the Hypershade, MMB drag the new Lambert shader with the label image on it to the work area in the Hypershade. Select the shader, and click the Input and Output Connections icon (shown here at left) at the top of the Hypershade window.

5. Your Hypershade should now look like Figure 3.14. Notice the node icons are connected by various colored lines. These show the connections between nodes that make up the shader and the ultimate properties of the rendered label. You'll see an icon of the wine label image file named *file1*. Double-click that node. In the Attribute Editor, click the place2dTexture1 tab to get access to the attributes of the *placement node* for that file image node.

6. In the Attribute Editor for the placement node, set Rotate Frame to 90 to turn the label right side up. But wait! The label is inverted; it's a mirror image of itself. This is more a function of the surface than of the placement of the texture though.

Surfaces have a definite direction, a source and end point that are defined by the CVs (control vertices). Surfaces also have normals that define which side of the surface is outside. Most modeling programs don't really pay attention to the "inside" side of a surface; they don't need to render it. Why waste the processing power on something that won't be seen? That's where normals come into the picture.

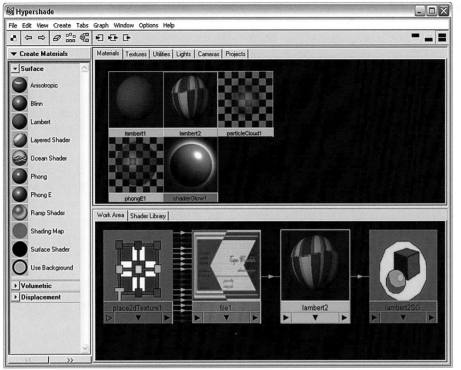

Figure 3.14: The shader network for the wine bottle label

By defining which way the normals of a surface face, you tell the computer to render that side. Most current 3D applications default to making surfaces double-sided, so it's not so much an issue which way normals face—until you find your textures mirrored like our wine label.

7. We need to flip the normals over to the right side. Choose **Display → NURBS Components → Normals (Shaded Mode)** to specify which way the normals face. You should see nothing, really, as all the normals will face into the bottle.

8. Flip the normals by choosing (in the modeling menu set) **Edit NURBS → Reverse Surface Direction ❑**. In the option box, set the Surface Direction option to U. It so happens on this surface you'll need to switch the U direction. Usually you try one direction to see if it works, undo it, and try another direction until it works. Click Reverse. The normals pop out and face away from the label, and the texture file flips to being normal. Turn off the normals again by choosing **Display → NURBS Components → Normals (Shaded Mode)**.

You can check your work by opening the scene file `Bottle_Texture_v03.mb` in the Wine_Bottle project to see how it compares.

Adding Surface Detail

Now that we have mapped on the image, we can get a little jiggy with it and add some surface detail through the Label shader's *bump map*. We're going to raise some elements on the label by creating a Photoshop image from the original label and applying it to the shader. A bump map creates the illusion of surface texture (like ridges or bumps) by rendering highlight and shadow. For that, you assign a black-and-white map or image file to the shader's **Bump Map** attribute. The lighter areas of the image raise the surface detail; the darker areas lower the surface.

We'll start in Photoshop to create the bump map image.

1. Open Photoshop, and load the `wine_label.tif` file found in the sourceimages folder of the Wine_Bottle project. Our purpose here is to use the primary design elements to create raised and lowered elements in the label itself.

2. First desaturate the image to create a black-and-white file. In Photoshop, choose **Image** → **Adjustments** → **Desaturate**.

3. Now open the Levels Adjustment window to adjust the brightness levels of the label to create some nice contrast. Choose **Image** → **Adjustments** → **Levels**. Make some adjustments to crush the brightness range to match Figure 3.15. This will make for a nice bump image.

4. Save the file as `wine_label_bump.tif` in the sourceimages folder with the original color map file. It's important to maintain a good naming convention as you work so that you know immediately which images go together for a shader. Later you'll see how to effectively use a PSD file to keep everything contained in multiple layers in one Photoshop file.

Figure 3.15: A good contrast image will make a good bump map for our label

5. Back in Maya, double-click the lambert2 shader that is the wine label's shader, and rename it wine_label. In the Attribute Editor, click the map button next to the **Bump Mapping** attribute, and create a new file texture node, as you did with the label's color. This time, select the `wine_label_bump.tif` file we just saved in Photoshop.

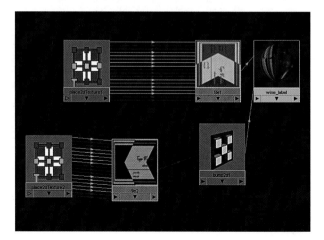

Notice how the bump image is oriented incorrectly as the original color map was before we rotated it to 90. We can always go into the texture placement node of the bump map and rotate it 90 as we did with the color node, but let's try something a little more clever. We're going to connect the placement node of the color image file node to the bump node. This way the settings that are already in place for the color image placement will be on the bump map image placement as well. Furthermore, any changes you make in the placement of the color map will affect the bump map, so you don't have to change both manually.

6. Simply select the bump map's texture placement node and press the Del key to delete it. Then MMB drag the color map's texture placement node on top of the bump map image node. When you release the MMB, choose **Default** from the pop-up menu to make the connections. Voilà! Whenever you change the placement of one, the other follows.

7. Now when you test render, you'll see the label is looking a bit frazzled. The bump map is too severe, as you can see in Figure 3.16. You can solve this problem in two ways. You can use Photoshop to reduce the contrast in the image, since contrast is what creates the amount of bump. Or better yet, in the Hypershade, double-click the bump2d1 node, and turn Bump Depth down to 0.15.

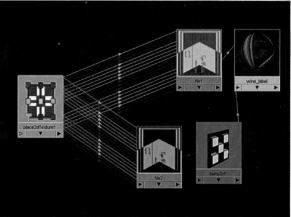

8. But the image still looks as if the bump is going the wrong way, meaning the name of the wine is pressed into the label as opposed to popping out a bit. This you can also fix in Photoshop or in Maya. In Photoshop, you can invert the image so that the black becomes white and vice versa. But guess what? You can do that in the Maya file image node just as easily. Double-click the file2 node that holds the bump image, and in the Attribute Editor in the Effects section, click the Invert check box to turn it on. You'll notice the bump map inverts. Now if you render out, the label resembles the one in Figure 3.17.

Figure 3.16: The bump map is too high.

Figure 3.17: A subtle bump map can go a long way.

Wine Bottle Part Deux

In this exercise, you'll use polygonal UVs to map a Photoshop image to the bottle's label and learn how working back and forth with Photoshop layers lets you map several attributes to the label with only one PSD file.

Load `Bottle_Poly_v01.mb` from the Wine_Bottle project on the CD. In this scene, we have the same bottle we worked with so far, but the label is now a simple polygon model. This exercise is to get you acquainted with how Photoshop can make short work of polygonal texturing.

Part of the difference between texturing a NURBS object as we just did and texturing a polygonal object has to do with how UV coordinates are defined. The wine label on this bottle is made of polygons and will have a bit of a different UV layout than the NURBS label we just finished. To that end, we'll use Photoshop to place our new label.

Texturing the Label in Photoshop

To texture the label, follow these steps:

1. Open the Hypershade and create a new Blinn shader. Our label will be glossy. Assign the new blinn1 shader to the label.

2. Now instead of starting to import images for the attributes we'll be mapping, we'll write out a PSD file as the template. Select the label in Maya, and (in the Rendering menu set) choose **Texturing → Create PSD Texture** to open the Create PSD Texture Options window, as shown in Figure 3.18.

3. We'll have to decide how large a canvas we want in Photoshop. Most textures are typically square, for example, 1024 × 1024 pixels. Since our label is essentially a rectangle wrapped around a bottle, we should enter 1024 × 512 for the **Size X** and **Size Y** attributes. Make sure Include UV Snapshot is checked. At the bottom of the window, you can select the attributes of the shader you want to map and subsequently attach to this new PSD file. Select **Color**, **Transparency**, **Bump**, and **specularColor**, and click the right arrow to move those attributes into the Selected Attributes box, as shown in Figure 3.18

4. Click Create, and Maya writes out a PSD file in the sourceimages folder of your current project, which should be set to Wine_Bottle. By default, the filename will correspond to the filename of the scene and the name of the surface, though you can change it in the Create PSD Texture Options window. We'll leave it at the default.

5. If you take a look in your project's sourceimages folder, you'll see a PSD file called `Bottle_Poly_v02_poly_labelShape.psd`. Open it in Photoshop. The file will contain several layer folders, each corresponding to the attribute involved. You will also notice a grid, as shown in Figure 3.19.

Figure 3.18: The Create PSD Texture Options window

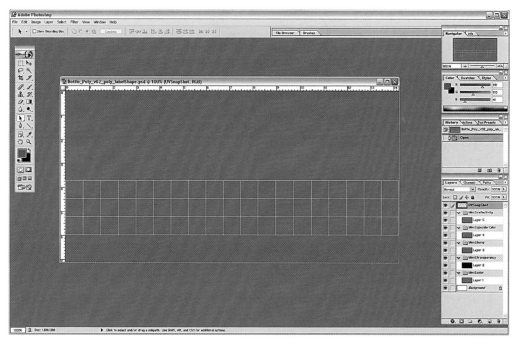

Figure 3.19: The PSD file shows the UV grid of the wine bottle label as well as a layer folder for each attribute.

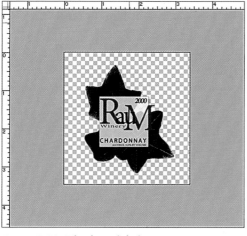

Figure 3.20: The front label

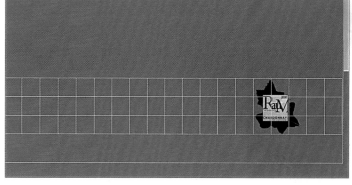

Figure 3.21: The front label pasted into the Photoshop texture file

The grid is the UV layout for the surface. Since this is a simple surface, the grid is straightforward. The more complex the surface, the more helpful the grid will be for painting the textures. Nonetheless, this simple grid is a big help since it tells us exactly where on the Photoshop canvas we should paint.

6. We'll use graphics contained in another Photoshop file to paste together our texture maps. Open the file Raum_Winery.psd in Photoshop, as shown in Figure 3.20. Select All, and copy the image. In the texture file, paste the label image to the blinn1.color folder. You'll have to turn off the other layers to see the image, though you should leave the UVSnapShot layer turned on. Scale it down, and place the image to show something similar to Figure 3.21.

7. Back in Maya, choose **Texturing** → **Update PSD Textures**. Open the Hypershade, and MMB drag the blinn1 shader into the work view. With blinn1 selected, click the Input Connections icon (shown here at left), and you'll see that the blinn1 shader already has four connections. When you wrote out the PSD file, Maya automatically made all the proper connections for you, as you can see in Figure 3.22. You will notice that one of the file nodes now displays the wine label graphic in gray. The others are either gray or white. We still need to play with those layers in the Photoshop file.

8. In the perspective view, press the 6 key to enable textured view. As you can see in Figure 3.23, the label graphic is on the gray label. Notice how the graphic is squeezed in the sides. We need to stretch it out in Photoshop to get the proportions right. If the perspective view does not show you the graphic, make sure Hardware Texturing is enabled. In the persp view panel, click Shading, and make sure Hardware Texturing is checked.

9. In Photoshop, stretch the graphic horizontally. Although it may look stretched in the Photoshop image (see Figure 3.24), it will look in proportion when it maps (see Figure 3.25). This is where the UV snapshot comes in handy. You can use the grid lines in the Photoshop file to line up with the grid of polygons on the label itself. You'll see that making the graphic about 3 grid units wide will work.

10. We're not looking for a gray label that wraps all the way around the bottle. Instead we want the front graphic to be a cutout label, so we'll adjust the transparency layer of the Photoshop texture file to cut everything else out of the label. In Photoshop, select the label's graphic in the blinn1.color layer, and copy it into the transparency layer folder, making sure the copy lines up with the original. If you turn off all the other layers, you'll be working with just the transparency now. The trick here is to create a black-and-white layer, in which white is transparent and black is opaque.

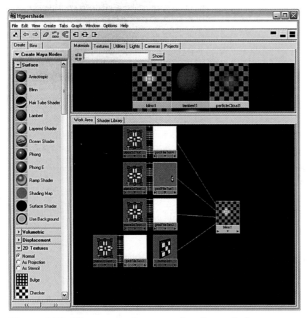

Figure 3.22: The connections are already made for you based on the layer folders in the Photoshop file.

Figure 3.23: The front label is squeezed on the label

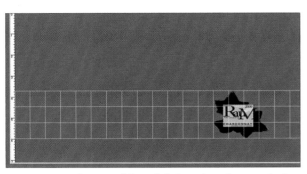

Figure 3.24: The pasted front label needs to be stretched.

Figure 3.25: The front label now looks proportional on the geometry.

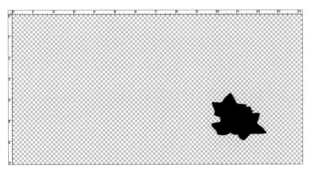

Figure 3.26: Create the transparency map.

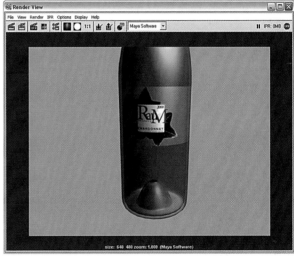

Figure 3.27: The transparent part of the label is still visible due to the highlight.

11. In Photoshop, choose **Image** → **Adjustments** → **Desaturate** and then **Image** → **Adjustments** → **Levels**. Adjust the levels until you get a black silhouette of the graphic against the transparent Photoshop background, as shown in Figure 3.26. You may have to use the Paintbrush Tool to clean up any areas of white inside the black silhouette and vice versa. Save the file.

12. In Maya, choose **Texturing** → **Update PSD Textures** again to update the latest changes. You won't see the transparency necessarily, so you will have to render a frame to see it working. Once you do, you should see something similar to Figure 3.27. Notice that the graphic is not affixed to the bottle without the rest of the gray label, but a highlight goes all the way around, showing the gloss of the transparent bits of the label. We will have to change the **specularColor** now.

13. In Photoshop, select the black silhouette of the transparency map and copy it. Then paste it into the blinn1.specularColor folder. Make sure the two align. The **specular-Color** attribute governs the highlight color of a surface. The brighter the specular color,

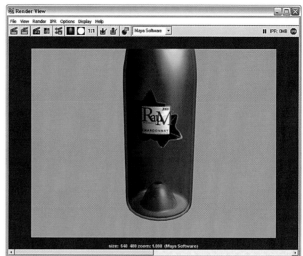

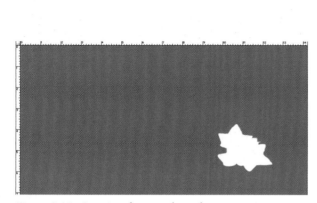
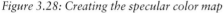

Figure 3.28: Creating the specular color map

Figure 3.29: The label with the proper specular map applied

the glossier the surface will seem. We want to map this attribute so that there is no specular highlight where there is supposed to be no label. A specular of black will give no highlight, so we will need to invert this image layer so that the label graphic is white and the surrounding area is black. In Photoshop, choose **Image** → **Adjustments** → **Invert**. The graphic will turn white, as shown in Figure 3.28. But we still need black for the outside areas, so turn on the gray layer in the blinn1.specularColor folder. Adjust that layer's levels to get it to go black.

14. In Maya, update your Photoshop textures. Render a frame, and you'll see that the highlight around the bottle is gone, as shown in Figure 3.29.

15. Now we'll add some surface bump to the label to make the name pop out a bit. We'll be painting in the blinn1.bump folder layers to create the bump map. As you saw in the earlier bottle label exercise, a bump map bumps out with a color brighter than 50% gray and bumps in with a color darker than 50% gray. In Photoshop, turn on visibility for the blinn1.bump and its gray layer. In the blinn1.color layer, copy the graphic and paste it into the bump layer in front of the gray. Make sure the layers align.

16. Turn off all the other layers, and work in the bump layers. We want the letters "RauM" to bump out, so adjust their color properties to make the letters white and everything else gray. You may have to use the Paintbrush tool to paint in or mask out the areas, assisted with perhaps the Magic Wand tool in Photoshop. Try to get your bump layer to match Figure 3.30, then save the file.

17. In Maya, update your PSD textures. The "RauM" letters you've created for the bump layer will now make the letters on the bottle puff out. Use the bump node's **Bump Depth** attribute to control the amount of bump in the letters. A **Bump Depth** of about 0.1 should be fine. Figure 3.31 shows how the letters puff out.

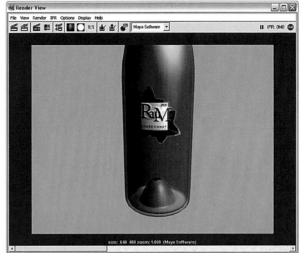

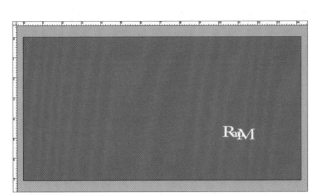

Figure 3.30: The bump map will bump out the letters only.   *Figure 3.31: The letters now puff out on the label.*

Creating a Back Label

Now to get a little more practice, use the graphic provided in the sourceimages folder to create a back label for the bottle using the same Photoshop file. You'll need to line up the layers properly in the Photoshop file to end up with the front label where it is now and the back label on the opposite side of the bottle. Be sure to create all the necessary layers so that the back label displays properly, as we did with the front label. This, in a nutshell, is some of the greatest interaction between Photoshop and Maya that typical CG artists will see.

Further Practice

Theory is all well and good, but until you get your hands a little dirty with some simple exercises, you can't really understand the concepts. With this chapter, we mapped image files onto two wine bottle labels, using two similar yet different techniques. In the first exercise, you became familiar with how file images are used to affect the attributes of a shader and what that all means to you and your image. In the second exercise, you explored some advanced techniques for keeping items organized by using a single Photoshop PSD file.

Now that your feet are wet, the concepts discussed in the rest of the book will be more accessible and understandable. Even though these bottles may not be the most striking images you can create with Maya and Photoshop, they showed you how the two programs work hand in hand, back and forth to create an end result.

two

PART

Striking Graphics for Various Markets

The world of illustrative artwork is evolving. As you stand at the open gate watching the scene unfold, artists are working with Maya and Photoshop to create stunning images for diverse, artistic realms. From the cover of *Time* magazine to brilliant ancient worlds on the Discovery Channel and in the Egyptian Museum, and from the corners of the web to the fast lane, the following pages reveal the dramatic creations that artists have produced from their own minds, as well as from past and present realities. The artists portrayed here have put the tools of Maya and Photoshop to work, fostering magnificent creations and rare beauty.

four

Dazzling Illustration

When it comes to *blending the strength of Maya and Photoshop with the power of natural and industrial imagery, Meats Meier has definitely found the right recipe. His otherworldly images and brilliant construction cross the line between mechanical nature and nature itself. Machines become organic structures. Metal takes on life. The essence of form is reduced to wireframes—not just 3D wireframes, but* actual frames of wire. *When you see it, you want to believe it.*

Meats's Road to 3D

Meats's artistic career shows a history of engaging an array of mechanical innovations, blending commercial viability with edgy design. As is the case with so many artists, it all started when Meats was just a kid. "My love of drawing and creating when I was younger eventually led me to find work as a T-shirt printer, which then turned into actually designing the prints themselves," explains Meats. "I eventually started creating my own line of T-shirt designs and sold quite a few of them out of my house and at a few shops at my local mall." (For the record, Meats's White Boy Desert Wear predates and has no relation with today's Whiteboy brand.)

With the desire to customize the screen-printed designs after they were printed, Meats became well-acquainted with the airbrush. Once he became airbrush proficient, he painted his truck in Moab style, covering the entire body with petroglyphs. The truck attracted lots of attention and lots of work. "From 1990 to 1994, I must have created more than 200 separate airbrush images while I was perfecting my skills," says Meats. "I had a lot of fun freelancing with my airbrush, painting snowboards, motorcycles, and automobiles, as well as covering my whole house in murals." But the love affair between man and airbrush was not to last. "As I began to learn digital painting and get into 3D, my airbrush quickly began to collect dust," shares Meats. "No more messy paint and clogged nozzles to get in the way of creative

dreams." In a sentiment shared with more than a few of today's digital artists, Meats adds, "I'm proud to say that I am now 100% digital."

Meats's leap from airbrush artwork to 3D and video games turned out to be a stroke of luck. Because he had created a lot of airbrush artwork for bands—illustrations for flyers, posters, and CDs—Meats's artwork was all over Salt Lake City. "As it happened, this guy who was starting a video-game company also owned a couple of bars," Meats recalls. "He called me up and hired me to learn 3D. It felt like lightning striking … the chance of that happening. The guy assumed I could do it and he was right. I picked it up quickly, and we both lucked out."

It's in the Wires

Although Salvador Dali may be best known for melting clocks, Meats Meier is perhaps best known for his wiry forms and intricate constructions. His style has been evolving for several years, having first appeared in the Etcher series, back in 2001. Early on, Meats began to notice that people recognized the wiry work as being uniquely his. "It's a rare thing in 3D to have a recognizable style," says Meats. Without a doubt, Meats's remarkably complex characters are instantly familiar. This is by design. "When I create artwork, I try to describe forms by using smaller, more intricate forms," he explains. "I have always had spiral, tubelike things in my artwork. They're 3D paint strokes, in a way." The wiry forms have been used in four or five series over the years, with roughly 100 pictures created for each series.

The Evolution of Mother Nature

With its trademark wire structures and dense construction, the *Mother Nature* series is unmistakably Meats. The series was created as a birthday present for Meats's wife. "Susan has a green thumb and is always planting things in the garden," says Meats. "I chose to represent Mother Nature as half human woman and half 'plant life.'" The result is unlike anything you've ever seen before. Mother Nature's main form was modeled in Maya with curves, which were then extruded into tubes. The tubes were then edited to provide a higher level of detail. Mother Nature's hair was created with Maya 5's Paint Effects tool (see Figure 4.1).

Paint Effects allows the artist to quickly create a high level of detail and comes with an array of premade brushes. Meats used the standard Paint Effects foliage and leaves as a stepping-off point, customizing the choices to fit his needs. The modifications were spur of the moment. Like Mother Nature herself, the plant-life Paint Effects evolved as Meats was at the point of creation.

Figure 4.1: Mother Nature

Sketching and Modeling

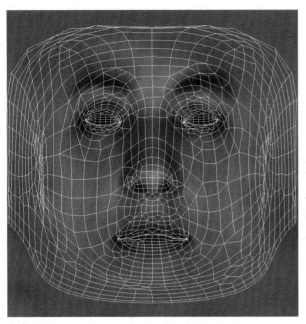

Figure 4.2: Mother Nature's UV face layout

The sketching process is an integral step in Meats's digital success. "As with all my 3D projects, I began Mother Nature in Photoshop, roughing out loose ideas until I was happy with the direction my idea was going," Meats reveals. "It is not unusual to have 20 or 30 sketches before I even open Maya." Once Meats has begun his 3D work in Maya, he renders test images to be brought back into Photoshop for experimentation. This methodology allows him to further develop and refine the concept, using sketches before tackling the more complex modeling tasks.

After the conceptual work is done, Meats goes back to Maya to finish the 3D modeling and lighting. Then it's back to Photoshop. "Once my 3D model and lighting is completed, I send the pretextured UV information to Photoshop, where my texture maps are painted," Meats explains. "I paint separate maps for the color, specular, and bump files." This process gives his images an extra punch. When the three maps are combined, the resulting images are much more detailed and realistic. Figure 4.2 shows Mother Nature's UV face layout as viewed in Photoshop.

Test and Final Rendering

Once the color, specular, and bump maps have been applied in Maya, Meats does a number of test renderings at low resolution. When everything looks right, it's time to create the final render. The final image is rendered at the highest resolution possible—in most cases 4096 × 4096 pixels per inch.

Meats is a firm believer in resolution: "The more pixels you start with, the more detailed the final image." This approach yields an image that will hold up for output at 13" × 13" for conventional print work when sent to an imagesetter or platesetter. It's beefy enough for large-format color inkjet output, as well. "I had a gallery for a while," recalls Meats, "and we created a lot of big prints. The 4096-×-4096-pixel TIFF files printed nicely at 40" × 40"."

Meats takes extra steps to achieve the highest quality output. Multiple renders allow a great degree of control over the final image. "I don't just render a single image, although I do a separate render pass for the diffuse, specular, and sometimes reflection for the greatest level of control once I combine them in Photoshop," Meats explains. This approach lets him add highlights to certain areas. Figure 4.3 shows Mother Nature's specular render, and Figure 4.4 shows the shadow render.

Masking isn't overlooked. Meats renders his images to contain two masks. The alpha mask (see Figure 4.5) is used to separate the images from the background for fine-tuning and layering purposes. The z-depth channel gives the depth information of the rendered subject. As such, the z-depth channel comes in handy when adding fog or depth of blur effects.

Figure 4.3: Specular render

Figure 4.4: Shadow render

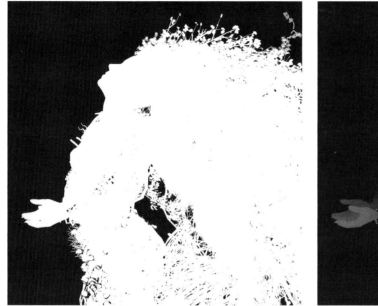

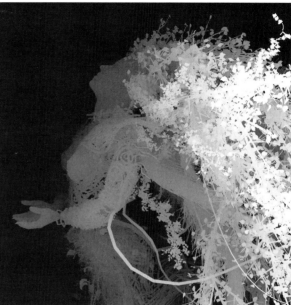

Figure 4.5: Alpha channel mask   *Figure 4.6: Z-depth channel mask*

With the z-depth channel mask (see Figure 4.6), things in the distance are darker, and foreground items are lighter.

Photoshop, Photoshop, and More Photoshop

After the rendering is complete—with all separate elements in hand—Meats launches into heavy-duty Photoshop mode. "I combine all my render passes and adjust the opacity and blur on each one until I am satisfied with the image," explains Meats. "Bringing a final rendered image into a 2D paint-and-post process such as Photoshop gives you a different kind of control, a per pixel level of control that enables you to fine-tune every aspect of the digital piece." It's these little tweaks that make the difference when you start viewing the image in full color (see Figure 4.7).

Sky's the Limit

Rather than build skies from scratch in Maya, Meats relies on the real world for his sky backgrounds. "I usually keep a digital camera with me at all times," says Meats. "When I see a nice cloud formation, I take a picture of it." Although Meats uses a low-resolution camera, it gives him enough images to work with. Once he brings a sky image into Photoshop, he enlarges it and combines it with other sky images. He continues to paint and combine, smudge and blur, and paint over until the final effect is achieved.

Meats uses an interesting technique to add a realistic appearance to sections of the artwork that need a bit of roughing up. "To add detail to areas that seem a bit too 'clean,' I find photographic textures and blend them into the image, erasing parts that don't fit well and cloning others that I feel add to the piece," explains Meats. "I try every blend mode with the added textures until I find one I like and that fits well visually. My favorite modes are overlay, hard light, and soft light, but I find that there is one perfect mode for every circumstance."

Texture Development

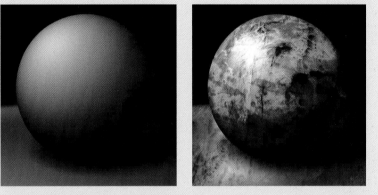

Most of Meats's textures are hand created. "That's just my personal way of doing it." He uses Photoshop's time-tested Offset Filter to achieve seamlessness. Meats simply offsets 50% on both axes to see the seams and uses the Clone stamp to paint over the visible seams.

With the technical work out of the way, it's time to put on the finishing artistic touches. At this point the image is nearly finished and is ready for the final detail, which is to create a painting layer and to use the Paintbrush to add the special details. Meats also fixes areas he finds look too "computery." "Coming from an airbrush background, this is my favorite part of the process, and it is the time when I feel the most like an artist." You can take the boy away from the airbrush, but you can't take the airbrush away from the boy (or something like that).

Figure 4.7: Mother Nature in full glorious color

There's just one more step in Meats's meticulous methodology before printing. To get a nice print from the image, he scales it even larger (200 dpi at 35" × 35") and spends some time looking for jaggies or stair stepping—"the biggest telltale sign of computer images," explains Meats. "I clean up the edges with the Smudge tool, blending the pixels to give the image a painterly look. I finish by giving the image a slight amount of grain for the final process." The final result (see Figure 4.8) is an image with a convincingly organic, rather than computer-generated, appearance. Adds Meats, "The Smudge tool is one of the most useful tools in correcting renders. It mixes pixels like the Paintbrush would."

The Evolutionary Process

In looking at the *Mother Nature* series, the evolutionary process in Meats's designs becomes evident. "I am creating as I model, building digital sculptures," he explains. "As I am doing it, I can see all the different paths I can take." This allows Meats to freeze a moment in time. "From there, I go on to the next step," he continues. "And by the time I am done with the series, I have a record of all the paths I have taken. I can look back from any one of the images and create a whole new series. It helps me remember where I went, where I was going." This is standard modus operandi for Meats, as each of his series can typically consist of 100 images.

There is much iteration in the Mother Nature series, with multiple renderings for each season of the year. Some display the lush flowers of spring and summer, and others show the stark, bare branches of winter. "I do a rendering and go on," he explains. "It's only later when I go back and look at all the different things I have rendered that I go back and add backgrounds—trying different colors all the way to the very end." This methodical process gives Meats an idea of what he wants for the final image.

Through the creative process, Meats rides the wave and goes wherever it takes him. He then goes back to look at what was created before moving forward. "Usually what happens," says Meats, "is that after one session of modeling, I take four or five high-quality renders and add backgrounds. The next day I start modeling, and adding on." He proceeds by working on the images in chunks. "I do not wait until the very end to finalize each piece," Meats explains.

Figure 4.8: Masked Mother Nature

74 CHAPTER 4 ■ Dazzling Illustration

On Learning Maya

Meats came to Maya while traveling down a converging path. The trail started back in 1994. "I was first introduced to Maya through its predecessors, the Advanced Visualizer package from Wavefront and the Power Animator package from Alias," explains Meats. "I was sent to SIGGRAPH in search of a great 3D program to design characters and animations." At the time, Meats was employed by a game developer, working on a fighting game. After seeing Wavefront's Advanced Visualizer, Meats made the recommendation to purchase the software.

For a path to converge, it must come from two locations. "Later, we acquired Power Animator, and for many months I was paid to get up to speed with both packages," says Meats. "After using both for a few years, the Wavefront and Alias joined forces and created their first version of Maya, which I was lucky enough to help beta test. I have used Maya for everything from package design to low-polygon game environments ever since."

Meats is realistic with regard to the length of the Maya learning curve. "Learning Maya (or any other 3D program) can be a daunting experience," Meats divulges. "Maya is a huge program containing many varying tools that can be used together to create pretty much anything you want, including your own movies and illustrations. Saying it is easy to learn would be an outright lie, but it can be mastered with a lot of hard work and dedication. Having all the power it provides to an artist makes the learning curve worthwhile. I recommend starting small and learning a small part of it at a time. Don't be afraid to try everything and learn everything that the program can do and then learn how to use it later."

Getting Better Mileage from 3D

Working in the 3D world opens corridors of creativity as it affords experimentation without the destructive nature of reworking artwork in a pixel-only (2D) medium. After you have gone through most of the work in creating the image, modeling it in Maya instead of drawing it in an illustration program, you have the ability to make several more images from your first, base image. "This process allows you to try your image with different lighting and camera angles. This gives you the ability to light and pose just like a photographer would." When asked why someone who is using Photoshop would want to take the leap to add 3D skills, Meats replies, "The third dimension also adds a whole new level of complication but adds a whole new level of opportunities."

"Now that I can sketch in 3D," Meats explains, "I am able to rotate my model in three-dimensional space and view it from every angle, instead of just two dimensions." In addition to enjoying the advantages of trying lots of variations in textures and lighting, Meats finds that the ability to pose with bones and controls is a huge benefit. The 3D process, as a result, is more akin to working with a living subject than it is to pushing 2D pixels.

The Internet has been a big positive for Meats's career. "The Internet is a great resource for students learning 3D. You can talk with industry professionals and newbies alike who can help steer you in the right direction and give you feedback on your works in progress."

Some of the sites Meats recommends include www.cgchannel.com for industry news, www.cgtalk.com for feedback in their forums, and www.highend3d.com for the endless supply of plug-ins and MEL scripts that can speed up the creation process.

Bio: Meet Meats Meier

Meats Meier is a self-taught, ten-year veteran of the digital arts who was named a Maya Master at SIGGRAPH 2003. His career has spanned the worlds of airbrush, T-shirt, video-game, print, and motion picture 3D design. Throughout it all, Meats's unique style has endured the changes in the medium.

"Being named a Maya Master in San Diego has been the high point of my career so far," says Meats. "I have always enjoyed learning about 3D, and art in general, and am 100% self-taught through a lot of trial and error. I find that just trying things is the best way for me to learn, so I spend a lot of time trying every way possible as my approach to solving problems."

Meats is currently employed as Technical Director at the Orphanage Inc. in San Francisco, California, with a focus on commercial and movie work. At the time we spoke, Meats was in the midst of belting out a series of 70-hour weeks doing special effects for the motion picture *HellBoy* (which was produced by Revolution Studios). Much of his work on the *HellBoy* consists of work with Maya fluids and particles. As the chapter wrapped up, Meats had begun working on *Sky Captain: World of Tomorrow* for the Orphanage.

Why "Meats"? His real name is Jim Meier, but when he was in high school, his friends took to calling him Meats, after a nearby restaurant called Meier's Meats. The name, like good animal protein, just stuck.

five

Classic Cartoon Sensibility in a 3D World

Toronto-based *guru animation studio (www.gurustudio.com) is a boutique animation house with a twist. Its forte is classic cartoon character animation. But instead of the time-honored, yet labor-intensive techniques of cel animation, guru's talented artists use Maya and Photoshop to bring the classic look into a 3D world. Their mission is to bring fabulous animation to the masses, as they aim to break down the barriers that have held back the medium and expand the market for innovative animated work. For founder Frank Falcone and the guru crew, it's not about the technology; it's about expressing an idea.*

In this chapter, you'll learn how guru created a set of short promotional animations (often referred to as shorts, interstitials, *or* bumpers) *for TELETOON, Canada's only French-and-English, 24-hour-a-day animation channel. A high level of Photoshop expertise enables guru's artists and animators to create warm, stylized environments and textures that avoid the cold look that chills many 3D pieces. Much of the work shown in these pages evokes the look and feel of classic Warner Brothers matte background cel animation, yet in a 3D environment.*

The 2D/3D Connection

In 2002, TELETOON called upon guru to create a series of promotional shorts. TELE-TOON had specific requirements for the pieces. "guru worked collaboratively with an illustrator (Ben Mazzotta) who understood the color palette and art direction that the network wanted," explains Frank. "The artist used his digital painting and illustration skills to draw detail into our rough sketches and layouts." The result is a fabulous series of more than two dozen shorts, each roughly 10 seconds in length. Not just any old shorts, mind you; these shorts bring all the crunchy goodness of the classic cartoon into today's digital world.

In writing this chapter, we had the good fortune to consult with Ben Mazzotta, the artist that created most of the artwork in Photoshop, Barry Sanders, the animator of the "Spider" bumper, and Max Piersig, the animator of the "Old Geezer" bumper. Multiple points of contact provide a great deal of insight into the process and the philosophy that drives it, with particular regard to guru's hybrid 2D/3D methodology. "Working with guru, I've discovered a niche derived from the need to '3D-ize' 2D images," explains Ben. "We're seeing this combination prevail more and more in 2D features and episodic television. Given the tools we have today, it's only fitting that 2D (still a very viable format today) has migrated toward the 3D realm."

The TELETOON Bumpers

Directed by Falcone and produced by Anne Deslauriers, the TELETOON bumpers pack a whole lot of lovely animation into just a handful of seconds. The running gag (to spoil the punch line) with each piece is to feature the TELETOON logo in a whimsical and unexpected place, as if to say, "Hey! If it's funny, it's TELETOON!"

The "Toaster" Short

Animator Jim Sayer

Background Artist Ben Mazzotta

The TELETOON "Toaster" short starts with anticipation and some classic squash and stretch. The lime-green kitchen has the feel of a golden age Warner Brothers cartoon in a 3D environment. Reflections in the toaster and ceramic tile backsplash and soft shadows on the countertop give the viewer the visual clues that this isn't their father's cel animation.

"Knowing that the toaster was going to be a 'character,' I supplied a reflection layer that could be placed offscreen and reflected in the toaster or texture-mapped," explains Ben. "This also meant that the palette could stay intact on the toaster as sometimes, various lighting effects on a texture-mapped 3D object can alter tones." Sticking with the TELETOON palette was essential. "This bumper uses a more extreme selection of the top and bottom tones of the TELETOON palette as many of the elements were chrome or generally shiny," explains Ben. "We also wanted a '60s retro feel for the spot, which is evident."

As the short begins, the camera angle looks slightly downward on the scene. The toaster stretches upward as it spews two slices of toast toward the ceiling at blistering speed. The scene quickly cuts to an upward shot of the ceiling, as if the viewer snapped their head to catch the rapid ascent of the toast rockets. A kitchen cabinet, a globelike ceiling-light fixture, and a roundtop refrigerator enhance the retro look.

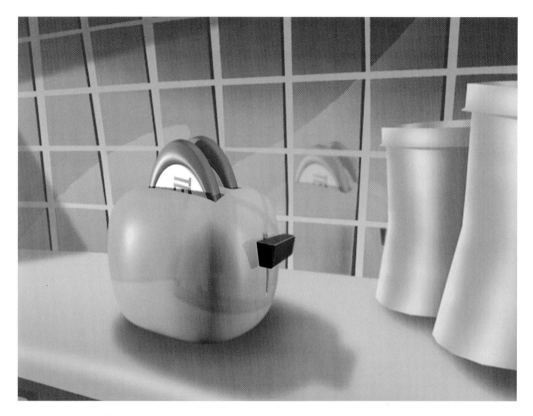

The toast flies upward into view, from the lower-left corner of the scene. The speed-blurred toast is visible for just two frames before it impacts the ceiling fixture. In the third frame, the fixture is askew, and the toast has ricocheted halfway across the screen. In two more frames, the toast is gone, and the ceiling fixture comes back into focus, as it rocks back, and cracks spread across its face. A handful of stationary frames allow the eye to recognize the result of the impact. The Photoshop file for this frame consists of a main layer with the light fixture and a crack on separate layers. It uses a basic rotation of the light with the crack appearing as it is hit.

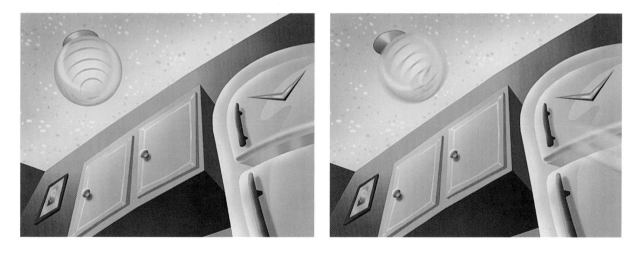

Cut to a shot of the checker-board linoleum floor, complete with a vintage chrome garbage can and a bowl full of dog food. The camera dwells a moment on the peaceful-ness of the scene before the toast rockets from the top-left corner of the scene toward the dog bowl. The toast slams into the dog bowl and ricochets off again, scattering chunks of dog food about the floor. The bowl skitters across the floor while the dog food flies.

An immediate cut to another upward shot, this one showing a big futuristic '50s wall clock, a sliver of wainscoting, and a doorway into the adjoining room, showing a table lamp and window beyond. The toast flies upward from the lower-left corner, toward the clock. When the toast hits the clock, the clock is sent spinning. Once again, the scene cuts rapidly.

A stainless-steel double sink is the focal point of the next scene. The left half of the sink is filled with dishes, pots, and suds. A sponge and a bottle of dish soap sit at the edges of the sink, and the bottom of the kitchen window is visible at top left. The toast flies in from the top right, slamming into the partially submerged plates, before ricocheting first into the bottle of dish soap and then off the top of the screen. As it does, the plates shift, the sudsy water splashes back and forth, and the dish soap teeters.

The dishwater uses a transparent layer atop elements at a transparency of 25 percent. "This was a difficult shot to layer mainly because of the dirty dishes in the sink," explains Ben. "The challenge was to achieve the water in front of and behind the pot and dishes while trying to conceal any overlap lines." A faint seam occurs when the front transparent water layer overlaps the back transparent water layer. "Even if you cut them to match perfectly, they can shift in animation and you see the seam," Ben continues. "I covered the overlap with suds so that when the dishes are hit, they bob up and down, sandwiched between water layers."

With another quick cut, the next shot looks slightly upward at another set of kitchen cabinets, complete with paper towel dispenser and cabinet-top knickknacks. The flying toast screams in from the left side and smashes into a cabinet door, knocking the door off its hinges and revealing the contents of the cabinet.

The final cut is superfast, briefly showing the kitchen window. The scene blurs almost immediately, as the first piece of blue toast flies into view from the top-right corner. The camera drops to focus on a plate at the kitchen table as the two slices of blue toast slam into the plate. As the plate and toast stop bouncing around, we see that the toast is in fact a TELETOON logo.

As the viewer's eye fixates on the logo, guru uses a subtle moving hold; heat waves rise upward in front of the window curtains, and the bushes sway in the breeze.

The "Old Geezer" Short

Animator Max Piersig

Background Artist Ben Mazzotta

In the opening scene of TELETOON's "Old Geezer" short, our aged protagonist is taking a peaceful stroll in the park, with the aid of his trusty walker. In the wink of an eye, he first lunges forward over his walker and then blasts backward as he flies into the air. The walker is flung forward, as the old man grabs his chest and stiffens, falling to the ground. A healthy amount of blur conveys the explosiveness of the moment.

Our octogenarian has barely come to a rest on the ground when the scene quickly cuts to a tight shot of a flashing red light on top of an ambulance. The buildings whiz by in the background, as the lights rotate and the highlights play across the bouncing roof of the ambulance and into the air. Adobe After Effects was used to juice up the siren scene. "I created the 'flare' with a solid layer that had a mask on it that was cut in the shape of the flash," Max explains. "Then I threw a bunch of effects at it 'til it looked right and squashed and stretched it to make it funny."

For this frame, Ben used a long, flat, seamless Cityscape layer to cycle in the background. Because the Cityscape layer uses a motion blur, it is rendered at a lower resolution. The sky and clouds were placed on a separate layer, which allows them to creep behind the cityscape (as it whizzes behind the ambulance).

Another quick cut takes us to the emergency room, as the doors swing shut. With this scene—shot from the floor—the green nature tones carried over from the opening scene take on a new meaning: hospital green. "We try to make the shots as dynamic as possible when it suits the context of the story," says Ben. "This shot is a good example. The Photoshop file consists of three layers: Foreground layer (ceiling, wall, and floor), Door layer (a straight-on, flat layer to be 3D-ized and slotted), and the Background layer (what you see behind the doors)."

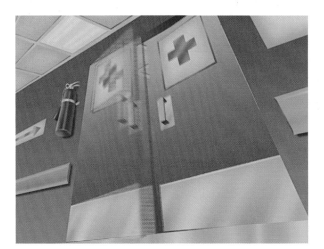

One more quick cut brings us to an eye-level view of the emergency room, with the doors at the right and a stretcher in the background. With just a few frames held, our octogenarian bursts through the swinging doors, magically full of life.

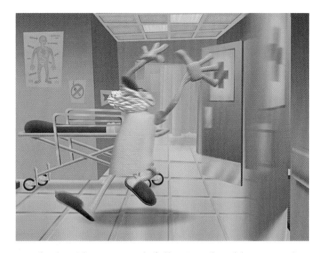

The camera dollies to the left as the old man dances a frantic, happy jig. Lots of blur imparts the feeling of motion, as he dances his way over to the X-ray machine, where he looks to be the model of health—both in skeleton and in flesh. "This is a three-cel-across frame, so that a sideways track following the old man to the X ray could be achieved," says Ben. "It uses the same Door layer as the previous frame, but with a perspective change. The long background layer has all the hospital fix-ins. The X-ray machine is placed on a separate layer with a hole cut where the X ray appears. I usually add a layer behind such cutouts so that graphics can be keyed onto it."

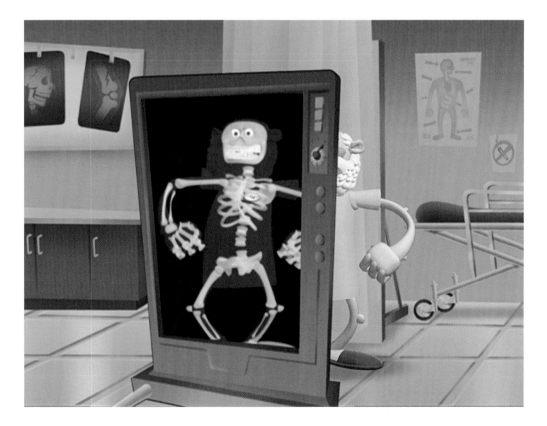

Let's take a closer look. A superfast zoom into the X-ray machine shows the source of the old man's new vigor. After Effects was used to impart the X-ray effect to the rendering of the bones.

The "Spider" Short

Animator Barry Sanders

Background Artist Ben Mazzotta

The TELETOON "Spider" short is a study in subtlety that pays homage to classic animation technique. The animator responsible for "Spider," Barry Sanders (www.barrysandersart.com), created the storyboard for TELETOON's approval before doing the layouts. After Barry created the initial drawings, the art was redrawn to match for the purpose of branding and color schemes.

Once again, Ben prepared the artwork in Photoshop and separated it into layers, with foreground and background leaves, and a web in the background, as well. Two texture maps are applied to every plane—texture map with image and the texture map to cut out that image. Alpha channels cut holes through the web for transparency.

Shot from above, the short begins with a bright green spider quietly minding his own business on his web, while raindrops fall. With the spider and his web in focus, blurred streaks in the foreground suggest another web closer to the camera.

A raindrop rolls down the big orange leaf at the top-right corner of the scene, bending the tip of the leaf in anticipation, as the raindrop rolls off. The raindrop lands directly on the spider's head below, spattering in all directions, while the spider looks upward with disgust and blinks. At some points, you can see the web wiggle. "I accomplished this by creating weighted clusters of points," Barry explains. "I put some motion on it and gave it a bit of jiggle. It's subtle, but it's there."

The spider retreats backward, scampering up his web, as the camera pulls back with a wonderful multiplane effect, thus revealing the web in the foreground. "I wanted to create parallax, in the way of Disney, with a series of moving planes," explains Barry. "It's a funny way to work, using a 3D program to create the illusion of 2D animation." Funny yes, but the technique works well for the "Spider."

As two raindrops roll toward the center of the upper web, they collide to form a TELETOON logo. The logo and web bounce convincingly to a halt while the rain continues to fall.

The raindrops are 3D objects that use a texture of green and white swirls, created in Photoshop. Backface rendering was turned off (a Texture Map option) on the raindrops to make them appear more realistic. "Think of it as a sphere," explains Barry. "With the ability to render the back side turned off, it looks more like an animated water drop." Once again, a simple trick creates a convincing effect.

"This spot was fun because it was like re-creating those amazing macro bug shots you see on the Discovery channel," says Ben. "As such, the sense of depth had to be taken to the max. Foreground and background layers were extremely blurred for the effect. I created two distinct web layers so that we could move out of one and into the one you see in the last frame."

Ben's Tip on Blurring

"As a background artist, I believe it's best to provide layers that you foresee as blurred, intact, and not blurred," Ben explains. "I usually hide these layers, copy them, and then blur the copied layers (and label them as TEMP) to give the 3D artists a sense of how much blur would look good. They can then adjust blur on the intact layers based on movement and virtual lens to really sell the depth they want to achieve."

The "Monkey" Short

Animator Allison Rutland

Background Artist Ben Mazzotta

The "Monkey" piece has a warm feel to it and features perhaps some of the most memorable character animation of the bunch thanks to animator Allison Rutland (www.allisonrutland.com). It begins with two monkeys on a tree branch, each with a banana in hand. The wooden fence in the foreground is initially in focus, while the monkeys are blurred. The camera focuses on the monkeys as it zooms in with a multiplane effect. As the monkeys come into focus, the fence blurs in the foreground.

"Knowing this was a push in on the monkeys in the tree, it was relatively simple on my end to achieve what guru wanted," Ben explains. "In a situation like this, you want a number of layers so that they can be displaced in time and space to achieve the sense of depth as the camera moves in. Blurring extreme foreground and background also allows for an artificial, midpoint, focal depth in the space, focusing attention on your characters."

As soon as the monkeys are in full focus, the scene immediately cuts to the monkey on the left. He peels his banana and eyes his monkey brother with extreme jealousy.

The camera rapidly pans to the monkey on the right. As the scene comes into focus, we see that the second monkey doesn't have an ordinary banana. No, he has a TELETOON logo!

The second monkey plucks the TELETOON logo from the banana peel and holds it up to behold. A fine logo, indeed.

Cut back to the first monkey; he's so entranced by the other monkey's TELETOON logo that he drops his banana before letting out a jealous shriek and scampering up the branch. A marvelous comic monkey battle ensues.

"These frames were pretty much a two-cel-across, rezed-up, and resized version of the wide," Ben explains. "As someone who's shot a lot of short films and videos, my experience with cinematography and, moreover, the use of lenses always comes in handy. I envisioned the first shot as seen through a 50mm, so it would follow that I would use an 80mm or 105mm for the close-ups. Camera angle and virtual lens change would bring the far background farther down and more out of focus." With the only camera move in these shots being the final zoom-in on the TELETOON logo, the Maya artist treated the tree branch as hybrid 2D to deliver a 3D appearance.

The TELETOON palette was used to effect a feeling of warmness. "This spot utilizes the top three hues (of five) in the red TELETOON palette to give the impression of day," Ben explains. "Slightly darker hues were used around the characters to frame them against the lighter background."

The "Sheep Factory" Short

Animators Andrew Kim, Jason Carswell, and Mark Cutler

Background Artist Howard Lonn

The TELETOON "Sheep Factory" short begins with the first sheep heading down the conveyor belt. In the background, the factory chugs along, providing visual interest in the form of secondary animation. The piece feels extremely fluid, as it takes place in one shot, with Maya's camera dollying down the production line. When the sheep reaches the end of the conveyor belt, the vacuum arm lowers itself and sucks the impossibly large and fluffy sheep into the nozzle. The ductwork bulges—like a boa constrictor that's swallowed a rat—as the sheep makes its way to the center of the machine.

The first sheep appears in the machine's view window as the second sheep reaches the end of the conveyor belt. The second sheep is vacuumed up, as the yellow light at the top of the machine flashes and the first sheep is simultaneously sent into the shearing bin. Maya's camera pans upward, as a frightening pair of augers are lowered into the bin. The gears on the machine whir, and the yellow light flashes again as the augers start spinning and the fur (literally) starts to fly.

Once the fur shower subsides, the augers retract, and the exit pipe swings outward while the camera pans downward. Maya's camera quickly zooms in and down as the first sheared sheep is deposited on the exit conveyor, revealing a TELETOON logo body. The exit conveyor starts as the sheared sheep shivers. A second and third TELETOON logo-bodied sheep are produced as the short ends.

How Maya and Photoshop Fit In

"Most animators at our studio have a strong knowledge of Photoshop before they begin using Maya," says Frank. "Some, though not all, could even be considered 'power users' [of Photoshop] but only if they had previously worked in a field that related more to illustration or graphic design."

guru Studio has found Photoshop's layers indispensable in production. They're especially fond of Photoshop's alpha channel controls and ramp tools: "Layers and alpha channels allow us to separate a drawing or an illustration into perspective-friendly components. By stacking foreground elements on top of background elements, we are able to break out these layers as separate images," explains Frank. "These separate images of the illustration can then be reconstructed in a 3D Maya file (or an Adobe After Effects file or some combination of the two), to create a multiplane camera environment whereby each layer is spaced apart in the Z axis away from the camera, so that any 3D camera moves will give the proper illusion of parallax and allow the 3D elements in the animation to live with the 2D elements in harmony."

How Much Resolution?

"Frame size is dictated by the amount of camera move," explains Ben. "An average cel is 1800 × 1350 pixels at 300dpi [dots per inch]. We use 300dpi so that the backgrounds can be used in print applications later."

"Our net effect is that the 2D images are drawn to look a little 3D, and the 3D elements we render out of Maya to match the stylized illustrative 3D look," says Frank. "To most viewers, the 3D should not be discernible from the 2D image layers." Careful attention to detail makes it all work.

"I try to make my backgrounds look fairly 3D as to not detract from the characters or juxtapose too much," concurs Ben. "Given the palette, it's necessary to use it in a way that gives as much depth as possible." When all is said and done, the audience has a tough time determining what elements are real 3D and what elements are pseudo-3D. These pieces are so fast, so brilliant, and so downright funny, the audience never has the chance.

In the TELETOON pieces, Ben used ramp tools extensively to create tonality and impart a sense of lighting direction in the 2D Photoshop layers.

Frank said the studio decided to go with Maya as its primary animation tool because it provides the animator with detailed, flexible, and interoperable character-rigging tools. "The character rig is essential for good, complex character animation. Without it, a character cannot be as expressive, and without tools that work quickly and seamlessly, we would spend far too long setting up characters, leaving us less time to animate and perfect the motion we create."

It seems like it's always crunch time in the animation world. Frank mentions that the studio engages in "creative reuse." It maintains a props database and a full character database in the studio "so we can go back and rip out a type of eyeball rig or a hand and repurpose or rework that model and rig to a new character that may have a similar design." Keeping production in full swing with time-saving techniques helps to ease the crunch, and that's one area where Maya's workflow and automation capabilities make it shine.

Company Bio: Becoming Animation gurus

Company guru

Location Toronto, Ontario, Canada

Website www.gurustudio.com

Staff 10 staff members and numerous freelancers

Founded 2000

guru animation studio sprung to life in 2000. Founded by Creative Director Frank Falcone and Executive Producer Anne Deslauriers, guru is both an animation production house and an original content creator. The studio has produced a healthy string of animated television commercials since its inception. Charm, liveliness, and a wonderfully comic sense are hallmarks of guru's work. As a boutique animation house, guru maintains a core staff while working with a range of freelancers chosen to meet the requirements of each project.

Not surprisingly, guru has racked up an impressive list of clients and awards. The studio's top-shelf clientele include consumer product giants General Mills, Hershey's, Kellogg's, and Kraft Foods and well-respected advertising agencies such as Leo Burnett, McCann Erickson, Ogilvy, and Saatchi & Saatchi. guru's directors have won awards that include a 1998 Clio Silver for Best Computer Animation (for Comdisco Chip) and a 2002 Ottawa Animation Festival First Prize for Best Station/Programme ID (YTD Promos).

Comic Strips in 3D

Damon Riesberg *uses the power of Maya and Photoshop to bring creative freedom to the production process of his comic strip "Syntax Errors." The combination of Maya and Photoshop speed Damon's work-flow, allowing him to focus on the characters and plot lines, rather than get-ting bogged down with the tedious and time-consuming chore of drawing and redrawing.*

"Syntax Errors" is worlds apart from traditional comic strip design, as it uses technology without compromising its creative core. In this chapter, we'll show you how Damon uses Maya and Photoshop to produce a daily comic strip. Damon pairs his creativity with his software knowledge to bring life to his characters. His unique workflow—while it represents a sig-nificant investment in research and development—greatly speeds produc-tion and revisions.

When I Grow Up, I Want to Be a Cartoonist

For almost as long as he can remember, Damon Riesberg has wanted to be a cartoonist. The dream began in second grade, when Damon put a pencil to his first cartoons. His aspiration stuck through his grade and high-school days, but it wasn't until college that Damon got his work into print.

While attending the University of California, Santa Barbara (UCSB), Damon penned "Sticks and Stones" (see Figure 6.1), a conventional comic strip for two college newspapers: the *UCSB Daily Nexus* and the *Sonoma State Star*. Although the comic strip ran for only a

Figure 6.1: *"Sticks and Stones" first saw the light of day in spring 1995.*

short time, the experience provided Damon with the opportunity to more fully explore the medium. Damon drew the illustrations conventionally—pencil and ink in a 20-inch format on Bristol board and reduced for print.

And Then, 3D Inspiration

It was at UCSB that Damon entered the world of computer graphics. "Our art department was very theory based, and I didn't think I'd ever be able to find a job with just theory," says Damon. "So I jumped at the chance to get into some computer graphics classes." Damon started with a couple of Photoshop fundamentals courses and some early web-development courses (which, back in 1994–95, primarily consisted of HTML scripting). He also worked with Adobe Premiere and Macromedia Director. "Those Premiere and Director classes had us doing animation, and that naturally led us in that direction," Damon explains.

As a third-year art studio and sociology major, Damon participated in a full-year 3D and animation class, which proved to be a crucial turning point for his career. With Wavefront Technologies headquartered in Santa Barbara, California, during this period, he was in the right place at the right time.

Alias Research was founded in 1983. Wavefront Technologies was founded the following year. The two companies merged in 1995 under the name Alias|Wavefront. The company changed its name to Alias in 2003.

The group of students were at a disadvantage, as animation expertise was sparse at UCSB. Although the students were encouraged to develop a story, the staff did not grasp what was possible with the software. Without sufficient guidance from the faculty, Damon and his classmates were off on their own. The team overshot on what they could accomplish. "We had no idea what was and wasn't possible in a nine-month class," said Damon. "We did three months of storyboarding. We planned on a nine-minute film and ended up with 30 seconds."

In a stroke of well-timed luck, Wavefront stepped in and kindly allowed the UCSB animation students to use a room at their headquarters along with computers and software for a year. "Mark Sylvester, the company's ambassador at the time, wanted to help the local community and wanted to get 3D animation in the schools," Damon explains. "One of the students in my group did a really great job with his animation the previous year (Alias|Wavefront sponsored a nine-month intro class at UCSB using Explore, Advanced Visualizer, and Kinemation) and was able to ask Mark if we could use the training room that they weren't using."

Explore and Kinemation were highly advanced and quite expensive at the time. Most other college students weren't nearly as fortunate and were stuck learning on far less powerful 3D software.

Damon and his classmates were able to use the room when the developers weren't using it, but they needed to keep a low profile. "We'd get into the training room, use their old machines, and work on TDI Explore and Kinemation for our projects," says Damon. "We only asked questions if we really, really needed to and even then kept them to a minimum. We knew we had a great opportunity—we all got a machine to work on whereas back at school, 30 people shared two machines. So, we didn't want to blow it by overstaying our welcome."

There were two UCSB teams with two projects. The teams got down to work and created some short films.

"We did whatever it took to get the job done," explains Damon. "I'm sure we were doing things in very unconventional ways but didn't know any better. If something worked, even if it took a long time, we'd do it that way because we knew it worked." Damon was part of two student projects that were ultimately shown at a number of animation festivals. One project was screened at both Spike and Mike's Sick and Twisted Festival and The Short Attention Span Festival. The other project was screened in the student section of the Santa Barbara International Film Festival.

After graduating from UCSB in 1997, Damon was hired by Alias|Wavefront as a technical support specialist. Alias|Wavefront must have been keeping an eye on the training room, after all. "Since we were there so much, (all-nighters were common the last quarter), I think they saw our dedication and at least got to know our faces," Damon says. "I met a few people there and had a friend from school (our TA in the class) who got an internship—so we did know a few people." When a job opened up, Damon applied. "Since they knew me and knew my work ethic, they gave me a chance."

At the time, Maya had not yet reached the market. "The great part about not having Maya experience," says Damon "was that *nobody* had any experience back then. Anybody that was hired had to learn."

From his UCSB experience, Damon came to know Explore and Kinemation well. He soon began training customers for Alias|Wavefront, both onsite and in the classroom. He spent a total of four and a half years in technical support, servicing movie studios and game developers. When Damon joined the company, Maya was still in beta. The opportunity to interact with an array of developers and clients allowed Damon to acquire a great deal of animation production knowledge.

Damon's stint at Alias|Wavefront ended in May 2002 when the Santa Barbara office closed. He used that time to start developing his comic strip, "Syntax Errors." During the spring and summer of 2002, Damon spent between 40 and 50 hours a week on his labor of love. Although some of the groundwork had already been laid, Damon used much of this time creating the characters in 3D.

"Syntax Errors" is a radical departure from the world of conventional comic strip design. "This is inventing a new technique for the medium," explains Damon. Although the production techniques break new ground, the subject is as familiar as Charlie Brown and his gang.

Creating "Syntax Errors"

"Syntax Errors" captures the exploits of four contemporary digikids (see Figure 6.2): Owen; his younger sister, Brie; and their friends, Rod and Rusty. True to comic strip kid form, the "Syntax Errors" kids are full of personality. Owen's most apt to ponder the big questions (and the big pictures), while the sweetly pugnacious pig-tailed Brie can't help but prove, over and over, how much smarter she is than her big brother. With his freckles and oversized spectacles, Rusty's an information-crazed cross between a young Bill Gates and Woody Allen. And (Hot) Rod? He's not just full of red meat and personality, he's full of himself.

Damon's characters are based on people he knows, but there's more to it than that. "In reality, they are all me too," he explains. "I can't write what I don't know about, so I put together some character traits from people I know and combined them into each character." Damon admits to borrowing specific jokes and creating story lines from real life. What's better than real life to inspire cartoon art?

The "Syntax Errors" kids have evolved over time. "They started with three fingers and a thumb," Damon explains. Unfortunately, this didn't have the Simpsonesque quality that was initially envisioned. "My friends saw it and said they looked like aliens," Damon continues. "So I went back and added another finger."

The "Syntax Errors" style is purposefully cartoony, rather than realistic. Damon feels that this is, at its core, an artistic choice. "I can do either with the toolset that Maya offers,"

Figure 6.2: "Syntax Errors" main characters Rusty, Owen, Brie, and Rod

Damon explains. "It just boils down to what looks better or what's more fun when shrunk down to the size of a comic strip. I'm choosing cartoony because I'd like it to be a fun comic strip. I think realistic characters that aren't exaggerated wouldn't be as fun to work on—or to read."

Where Maya and Photoshop Fit In

Like many cartoonists, Damon jots down his ideas for strips on whatever is handy at the moment inspiration strikes. This is a common practice. The difference is that Damon has his characters and environments stored in Maya, ready to be called into service at a moment's notice. "I can pose things quickly in Maya," says Damon. "The scenes are assembled pretty quickly. All I need to start is dialog or a story."

In creating the framework for "Syntax Errors," Damon's goal has been to create a comic strip in the least amount of time possible. Once an idea takes hold, he needs the ability to produce it immediately. The current benchmark is two hours from initial idea to finished artwork, but Damon is aiming to cut the average timeframe to just 90 minutes. With all the pieces in hand, the concept becomes reality.

Damon has knocked out a strip in as little as half an hour. This is possible when he's producing a series of strips with the same characters in the same environment. "The first one might take a couple of hours," explains Damon. "But every one after that is just reposing and rewording."

Photoshop is largely used as a compositing environment. He also relies on Photoshop for background colors and gradients. Although slight tweaks might be made to the renders, Damon primarily relies on "the religious use of Photoshop's layers" to speed the production process. He also uses Photoshop filters to add more contrast.

The production pipeline looks something like this:

- Four-panel framework exists in Photoshop.
- Text is dropped into each panel in Photoshop.
- Bubbles are drawn and sized in Photoshop. Once the bubbles are drawn, Damon knows how much room there is to position the characters in the camera view. "On my camera," Damon explains: "I've parented a templated set of curves that look like a big ticktacktoe board. It basically divides the frame in thirds, so I know easily where to place things in relation to the text in Photoshop (especially with Photoshop rulers and splices)."
- Individual frames are rendered as TIFFs in Maya.
- Each TIFF render is placed into its panel, with the renders placed on the bottom layer.
- Once a frame is rendered and placed, the render is checked and rerendered if necessary, to make the best possible use of space.
- After everything is perfect, the strips are rendered at 2430×832 pixels for print. The render is reduced to 710×243 pixels and saved for the Web as a GIF file in Photoshop.

Although Damon started with the traditional four-panel comic framework, he's recently started to experiment with ½ and ¾ panels to add a bit of diversity.

With a blank, four-panel framework ready and waiting in Photoshop, Damon is ready to go as soon as inspiration strikes. The frame template includes the strip title and website information (see Figure 6.3).

Text is set in Photoshop (see Figure 6.4). Although Damon started the strip using the Comix typeface, he has considered a change to a customized face.

Damon uses a set of more than 50 predrawn dialogue bubbles that he originally created in Adobe Illustrator. (He's constantly adding more bubbles to his library.) These bubbles can be quickly and easily modified to fit whatever dialogue is at hand (see Figure 6.5).

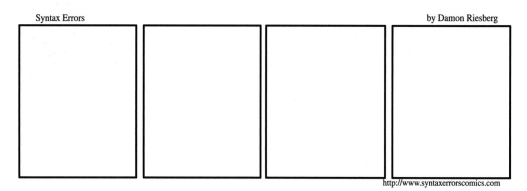

Figure 6.3: Framework in Photoshop

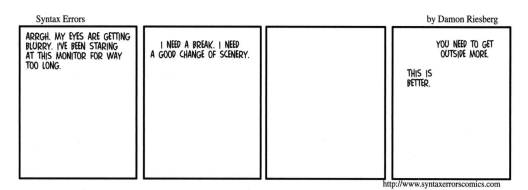

Figure 6.4: Dropping in the text in Photoshop

Figure 6.5: Drawing the dialogue bubbles in Photoshop

With the text bubbles in place, Damon can ascertain how to set up each render. His predefined camera settings make this a snap. "My camera has its render globals set to the proper frame size, so I always import my comic camera into my scene file," explains Damon. "In addition to the proper dimensions, my camera also carries a general light rig that is parented in the hierarchy with front, side, bounce, and shadow lights [see Figure 6.6]. The initial lighting gets me about 80% there, and it definitely saves me time because I don't have to create and reposition lights in every scene." There is considerable timesaving with this method. Damon estimates that he saves 30 minutes per strip by parenting the lights to the camera. Just as important, this arrangement provides a consistent look and feel throughout the majority of the "Syntax Errors" strips.

Figure 6.6: Lighting is carried with the camera.

Scripts save a great deal of time with character posing. "Ideally, I put a pose in my Pose shelf [see Figure 6.7], using a script that selects all my characters controls and another script that basically prints all its setAttr statements," he explains. "Then I copy that output and put it into my shelf." (The script is available from alias.com as well as from highend3d.com and other sites. It's been around for some time and was written by an Alias support guy a long time ago.)

Damon tries to save any pose that takes more than a couple of minutes to create. "It doesn't always work that way," he readily admits. "But I'm getting better at it, and it does save time." Damon's goal is to click a few buttons to get the character to roughly 70% of the pose, tweaking manually from that point.

Damon found that Maya's standard locators and selections handles offered room for improvement, so he designed his own custom posing and animation interface (see Figures 6.8 and 6.9).

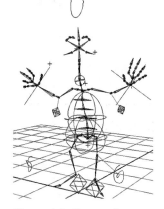

Figure 6.7: Damon saves various scripts for poses for each of his characters in a Pose shelf.

Figure 6.8: Custom locators and selections handles in wireframe

Figure 6.9: Custom locators and selections handles in preview mode

"I created my own curves for my posing and animation controls," Damon explains. "I created my own designs that are practical and easy to identify on each character. For example, I use a squiggly line for the knee pole vector control on each of my characters—it's just easier to see that it's a knee with my curves than with locators." Damon's knee control uses a templated curve that always runs from the knee to the knee control. This allows him to see exactly what that control belongs to, in any view.

Locaters and handles are shown as crosses by default. When tumbling in perspective view, the default handles can be difficult to see—it may be hard to tell which handle belongs to which control.

Saving Time with Naming Conventions

"I find that general optimization and organization is required for any pipeline to work efficiently," says Damon. Using a prefix for each character helps keep things tidy. "I try to name all the joints, controls, and shapes the same for each character," Damon explains. "Also, the layers are the same names, and I've only changed the prefix, so I know what is what. For example, Owen has 'o_bones' and 'o_geo' [shown here], and Brie has 'b_bones' and 'b_geo' for her layers." By keeping the titles concise, they fit into the Channel box; this makes them easy to read—a key to being quick in Maya.

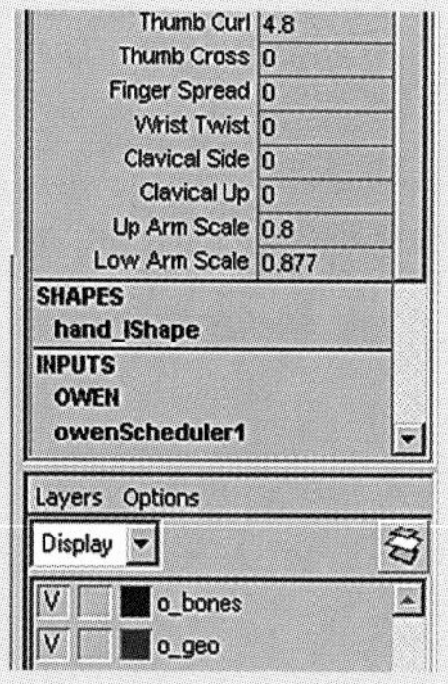

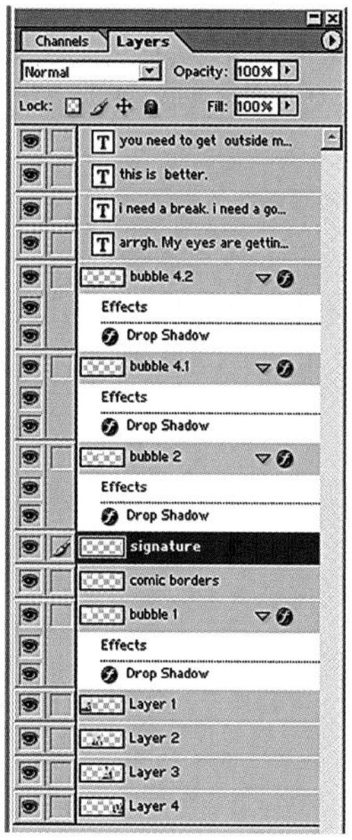

Figure 6.10: Lots of layers!

Final tweaks are made in Photoshop, as necessary. "Since my final result is 2D," Damon explains, "I can always use Photoshop to paint-fix things. This is sometimes a lot faster than trying to fix things in Maya." Damon continues: "I can fix shadows, backgrounds, and interpenetrations pretty quickly in Photoshop ... and I use that all the time." Photoshop is a great source for quick and interesting backgrounds—solid colors and gradients are a snap. Damon makes good use of Photoshop's web features, as well. "Save for Web and Web Colors are key for me," he says.

But all in all, Photoshop's layering capabilities are what make compositing the strip a snap. Most of Damon's strips come with a hefty Layers palette (see Figure 6.10). Figure 6.11 shows the rendered frames dropped on the bottom layer of the Photoshop file.

Figure 6.11: Placing renders in Photoshop

Figure 6.12: A change of scenery suits Owen in this completed comic strip.

If a panel is tight, Damon jumps back into Maya to make it all work. A slightly different camera angle may be all it takes. In just two hours from start to finish, the final four-frame comic strip rolls off the line (see Figure 6.12).

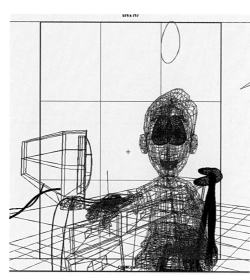

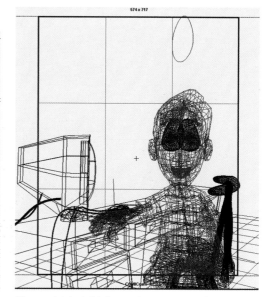

Figure 6.13: A frontal view of Owen in wireframe

Figure 6.14: A high-resolution view of Owen. Only what's inside the green box will be rendered.

A Pipeline Built for Speed

Damon constructed the "Syntax Errors" production pipeline to save time in the long run. He uses his deep understanding of the controls in Maya to quickly enable the posing and rendering of each scene. This next sequence of figures demonstrates how a typical scene is staged. First, we see Owen at his desk in complete wireframe, without the background and floor (see Figure 6.13). The joints are visible in the body, as well as some of Damon's controls.

Figure 6.14 shows a view of the scene demonstrating Damon's most common working mode. The grid is visible, but the floor and wall layers are hidden. A number of controls are visible, including the directional lights in the background and the wrist control locators. That's not a halo you see … the O over Owen's head is Damon's general control for Owen. "Each character has a letter that allows me to identify and move the character when the geometry is hidden and I only see the joints and controls," he explains. "I have the Overscan set higher than 1 on the camera so I can frame the picture better," explains Damon. "Basically, anything included in the green box will get rendered, but it really helps to see what else is close so I know where and how much I need to move things to get a good composition."

A parented lighting rig saves a great deal of setup time. "I don't have to light each and every scene," says Damon. "I just import the same camera (with my preset render globals that match my comic frames), and it carries the lights with it." The light rig has three lights hitting the subject from the front, a pair of back lights, and one bounce light. "I also have a shadow light in the rig that is point constrained," explains Damon. "It only translates and doesn't rotate (since the others are parented, they will translate *and* rotate), so it travels with the camera as well." Figure 6.15 shows a perspective view of Damon's comic camera (and parented lighting rig) in relation to the shot.

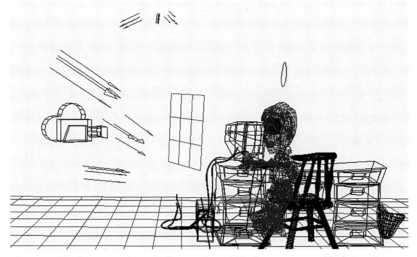

Figure 6.15: A perspective wireframe view with the camera and lighting rig.

Favorite Time-Savers

In addition to the time-savers already mentioned, Damon uses a number of handy techniques to streamline production:

- Blank four-panel comic borders are printed from Photoshop for use as pencil storyboards. The printed borders can be carried anywhere inspiration might strike. Characters are hand drawn as stick figures while in the brainstorming phase.
- Custom shapes and panels (circles, ¼ frames, ¾ frames, 2x frames) hide in the template layers.
- All the "Syntax Errors" kids are built with their feet on the ground plane, and backgrounds are locked with the ground plane.
- Damon models in polys, by choice. Because files are not output at a resolution that would derive benefits from NURBS, polys provide the benefit of speed.
- The camera is set to the exact size of an individual panel in Photoshop. It's not quite as easy as an Instamatic, but it's close. (Other Render Global presets are stored, as well.)
- Maya files are set up as 30-frame animations for standard 4-frame comic strips. Animations go from 0 to 30 and are rendered on 10s (0-10-20-30).
- Pose shelves help position the kids in an instant.

MEL Scripting Saves Clicks

As shown earlier with the Pose shelf, Damon believes in the religious use of MEL (Maya Embedded Language) scripts, and his animation settings are recorded in MEL. When he asks for a walking pose, for example, it's just a click away. Tweaks are added for individual shots. Although Damon also uses some keyframe and character setup tools, his biggest MEL scripting time-savers deal with smoothing and import issues.

"Since I work mostly with polys, I created a polySmoother that deals with the resolution of the scene," Damon explains. "It has three rows of buttons with three buttons each. The first row deals with all the polySmooth nodes in the scene—so I can hit 0, and it will force all smooth nodes to 0—hence, low res," Damon continues. "I can up it to 1 and 2 as well. The same is true with selected objects. I can make selected objects high res or low res with the click of a button. I also made it so I can add polySmooth nodes to objects and set their divisions to high or low or 1-2-3."

A simple file importer script streamlines input. "It's a pretty stupid script," Damon freely admits. "But it saves me a few minutes each time I load something. It's just a UI with different characters, locations, and the camera that I can import what I want at the click of a button."

On Learning Maya

A basic statement describes how Maya works: it's all about *nodes with attributes that are connected*. But this basic phrase can take a while to sink in fully. For Damon, it took a bit of time for everything to finally click.

"The best way to learn is to make your own project," Damon explains. "Standard tutorials do not teach you how to get yourself out of a bind." By creating your own project, you are driven to form your own solutions, rather than mechanically following a step-by-step tutorial. "When you first start tinkering around, do whatever it takes," says Damon. "Start with a final defined look, and then work toward it. This will force you to solve the problems."

Solving problems is where learning starts. "In most projects, the problem solving takes the most time," Damon explains. "So get used to it and get good at it."

Use Maya's feedback to help absorb what's happening. "Back when I was learning, I kept Hypergraph open to see what happened," explains Damon. "I'd refresh up- and downstream connections enough to become familiar with it." Does familiarity breed productivity? "There's an initial fear from people when they originally look at the Hypergraph," shares Damon. "To see it all the time, the fear goes away."

For many, Damon says, "the concept of 3D space is tough to get the mind around." Even more so, learning Maya is an ongoing commitment. "Stay with it," Damon continues. "Because Maya is so big, you may not be able to pick up where you left off if you go away for three months."

Other 3D Comic Strips?

Although a lot of other 3D comic strips are on the Web, there aren't a lot of great ones. Much of what's out there is on the lower end of the 3D complexity scale. Just as important, a good number of projects seem to be abandoned. It appears that a good bit of what's out there and active today has been produced with Curious Labs Poser.

There is, however, a 3D Comics Ring. Like most web rings, the 3D Comics Ring is constantly changing. Your best bet to find the ring is to Google "3D Comics Ring."

"Syntax Errors" Gallery

You can see more of Damon's "Syntax Errors" comic strips at www.syntaxerrorscomics.com.

December 1, 2003

January 26, 2004

January 30, 2004

Why Not Animate?

As far as "Syntax Errors" turning into an animated piece, it would seem that possibility might be a ways off. "Everybody asks me why don't I animate it, especially since I've got the controls and the power to do so," Damon said. "Well, time is one big factor. I've got a 50-hour-a-week job that needs to pay the bills. What I see before animation is going more days a week. I'd rather do that first. Then I can think about animation."

Bio: Damon Riesberg

Damon's Maya expertise earned him a spot with PDI/DreamWorks, where he works in the Clothing/Finaling department. Although Damon now spends time with "Syntax Errors" in the evenings and weekends, it's *Shrek 2* that's most recently taken his full attention weekdays.

Clothing and finaling are two key steps in the quest for a realistic feel. "For the clothing part, we do all the dynamic cloth simulations for *Shrek 2*," explains Damon. "This means clothes, capes, flags, banners, napkins, curtains, some hair simulations, and anything else that might look good controlled by dynamic cloth." In other words, flapping in the breeze is a good thing.

Finaling adds realism to a movie. "We work on collisions, interpenetrations, extra motion, and cleanup for the shots," said Damon. "Essentially, an example of what we do would be if somebody touches their face with their hands. Well, the fingers can't really push the skin around so our department would go in and make those deformations after the animation is already done. This allows the movie to feel more real, while not having to spend years on developing a rig that would accommodate any motion that the animator might do."

seven

Creating Realistic Animals: Bringing Dinosaurs to Life

The wizards *at Meteor Studios specialize in breathing life into their subject matter—whether the subject is long gone or yet to be built. From extinct beasts, such as the Tyrannosaurus rex, through extreme feats of engineering, such as the Bering Strait Bridge, Meteor imparts an incredibly realistic feel to their projects. It should come as no surprise that in just a few short years, Montreal-based Meteor has grown to be one of the largest animation studios in Canada. In this chapter, you'll learn how Meteor used Photoshop and Maya to re-create a dinosaur known as the Orodromeus for the Discovery Channel special,* Dinosaur Planet.

Creating the Orodromeus for *Dinosaur Planet*

The long-legged Orodromeus appears for approximately 5 minutes in a 48-minute production of Meteor Studio's acclaimed *Dinosaur Planet*. The episode "Lil Das' Hunt" takes place in prehistoric North America. Meteor kindly offered us the opportunity to interview their lead texture artist, Christine Leclerc. Christine heads up Meteor's fabulously talented texturing team on all productions. Prior to *Dinosaur Planet*, Christine led the texture artists on Discovery Channel shows, including *When Dinosaurs Roamed America* and *Before We Ruled the Earth*. Christine's background includes a degree in industrial design from the University of Montreal, ten years in exhibition and commercial design, and stints with a gaming company and on the television series *Excalibur* (TVA International).

Meteor's character designers began the project by studying references of the animal (see Figure 7.1). The designers prepared anatomical layouts and a full-color design based on the best research of today in close collaboration with renowned paleontologists. The designers

Figure 7.1: The reference design

studied the most minute details of the dinosaurs' fossil bones, teeth, skin, footprints, hair, and other attributes. Every element they can find serves as reference material to establish the look of the creature.

The designers also looked at present-day animals, to draw analogies in behavior and habitats. These represent an excellent source of inspiration for how a dinosaur would move within its environment. They also took into account whether the animal was a predator, a plant-eater, or carnivorous and where that creature lived, perhaps in the savanna or in the jungle. The anatomical layout was then given to the modelers in order to sculpt the shape of the creature. Texture artists used the full-color design as a reference to create all aspects of appearance such as color, wrinkles and folds, hairs, shininess, and so on to give the illusion of life to the creature.

Just creating one character is quite a time-consuming process. According to Christine, it took the designers a week to create the character design for the Orodromeus. The modeler and character setup artists took about two weeks each to complete their tasks. The entire process of texturing (including the UVs unfolding) consumed three weeks. The textures of the male were created first, with some of the maps subsequently altered to create the female and juvenile Orodromeus for an entire herd shown in the episode. "Within a couple of months, after checking on a turntable if everything is fine, the creature was ready to go!" Christine says. After all that work, how much screen time do the Orodromeus get? A mere 5 minutes. While Lil Das (a charming, yet dangerous young male Daspletosaurus) is the star of the show, the Orodromeus are relegated to a supporting role.

Stalking the Orodromeus: Modeling an Extinct Creature from Scratch

As the Daspletosaurus pack stalked the Orodromeus, Meteor's crew pursued the creatures in the quest for accurate modeling and vibrant animation. Christine explains that the Orodromeus, whose name means "mountain runner," is part of the Ornithopod family. "It was named by paleontologists John R. Horner and D.B. Weishampel in 1988," she says. "The Orodromeus lived during the late Cretaceous period about 77 to 73 million years ago in North America. Fossils have been found at Egg Mountain in Montana." Research suggests that the Orodromeus probably lived in a social herd, with a herbivorous lifestyle.

Figure 7.2: Wireframe model

According to the DinoViewer on Discovery.com, the Orodromeus makelai was approximately 8 feet long and 3 feet high and weighed in the neighborhood of 110 pounds. "Their lightweight bodies and long legs made the Orodromeus fast runners. They were the gazelles of the dinosaur world," says Christine.

Because of the complexity of the creatures, the model for one Orodromeus was one polyset of approximately 40,000 polygons (see Figure 7.2). The inside of the mouth was an entirely separate piece, as were the claws and teeth. The skeleton was composed of 116 joints. "We didn't use a muscle system for this creature as we often do for species with bigger musculature, a T.rex for example," Christine explains. They did create a custom jiggle deformer tool to automatically create secondary muscle wobble animation.

Skinning the Orodromeus

Christine considers skin appearance one of the most important aspects when texturing dinosaurs. "Impressions of dinosaur skin that have been found fossilized in ancient rocks show a thick, tough, and scaly skin. The presence of scales is important if we want to be accurate to the paleontologist discoveries." So, that's where they start—by covering the entire creature with scales of different size and function. For the Orodromeus, the artists drew bigger scales along the spine for protection purposes similar to what you see on a crocodile's back. Today's animals served as inspiration throughout the process. "Reptiles and chicken feet were used as references for designing the bottom of the legs, while pictures of birds were the base material for the beak," says Christine.

Research suggests that the Orodromeus was a fast runner and plant eater, so the designers based the color scheme on that of a gazelle. The designers chose earth tones, with a warm sienna as the main tone of the textures to integrate the Orodromeus better in his surroundings, which were created from shots of New Mexico. A bit of blue in the stripes provides an interesting contrast for the back of the Orodromeus.

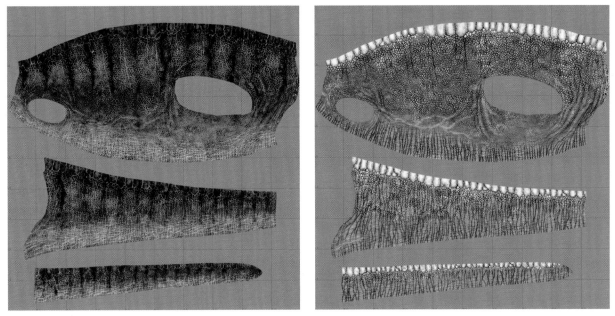

Figure 7.3: Orodromeus body skinnings

Figure 7.4: Orodromeus body bump maps

The Orodromeus model contains approximately 20 textures. Each major section of the Orodromeus model (the head, body, legs, eyes, and claws) required a set of four textures: a color map (see Figure 7.3), a bump map for cracks and creases (see Figure 7.4), a specular map for the shininess of the skin, and a displacement map for the bigger folds and scales.

Where Photoshop Fits In

Meteor's texture artists find the most delicate processes in Photoshop are done with layers, using modes such as Overlay and Soft Light. "The layers allow us to paint tons and tons of details independently and manipulate them easily. Also, mode layering can create great, rich, and subtle effects," Christine says.

As for Photoshop's tools, the various brushes give the artists the ability to hand paint. They use the Stamping tool to clone small samples and reproduce them on the entire surface and to make quick touch-ups. Rather than rely on third-party tiling plug-ins, the artists create seamless textures with Photoshop's built-in Offset filter.

As a result, Meteor's texture artists hand paint and customize most of the textures. "The details for the organic textures need to be precise, specific, and adapted to the creature that we are doing," explains Christine. The artists might use scans as a base for some details, but most often they cover and tweak the scans with so many touch-ups that the resulting artwork becomes an original creation. The texturing work has been exhaustive. "So far, we've textured as many as 60 species of creatures, not to mention the variations within the same species for females, juveniles, and babies," says Christine.

Hand-painted, detailed texturing was especially critical for the Orodromeus' head (see Figures 7.5 and 7.6), which appeared in many close-ups.

Because the artists do so much custom work, they often cannot share textures between creatures. Christine says: "All our textures are specific and custom-made for each animal. If

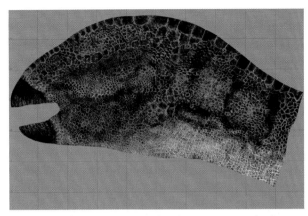

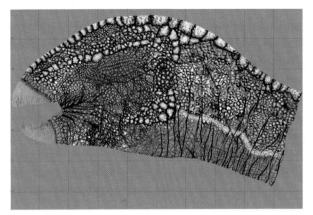

Figure 7.5: The Orodromeus head textures use a higher level of detail for close-up shots

Figure 7.6: Orodromeus head bump map

there are some similarities between two characters, we might reuse, for example, a layer for the base of the skin or the same pattern for the scales. But all the folds, the cracks, the color pattern that defines the look, and the personality of the creature had to be specifically tailored for him."

Eyeing the Orodromeus

The Orodromeus' eyes are truly spectacular and realistic. The model is composed of three parts. First, a sphere is made for the eyeball. Within it, a concave shape is then modeled for the iris on which they paint the color of the eye. They then duplicate another sphere slightly bigger for the gloss and the reflection of the environment in the eye. Christine says, "For the Orodromeus, the reflection is mostly what we see since the iris is very big and dark colored. The intention was to give an inoffensive and harmless look to the face of the animal, a bit like a cow." (See Figure 7.7.) The end result is both familiar and friendly.

Finishing Touches

Although the unfolding process is sometimes described with a dress pattern analogy, Christine says it's more along the lines of skinning an animal. The skin is unwrapped from the body to obtain a flat surface. "It's exactly the same idea when we unfold a model. The UV set represents an exact portrait flattened on a 2D surface of the 3D model," she explains. This way, you can have a system of reference between the 3D model and the 2D textures in Photoshop. You need that reference to paint precisely at the good location on the different parts of the model. Christine says, "For example, if you have to paint wrinkles on the neck, you'll find where to paint them on the snapshot of the unfolded UVs. So when you wrap the textures on the skin of the model, the wrinkles should lay exactly where they have to." A set of Orodromeus leg skinnings are shown in Figure 7.8.

To add color and displacement to a model in Maya, you must use a shader, which is a texture manager and a connector that contains properties and parameters for all the surfaces: color, bump, transparency, and so on. Christine explains: "Basically, you create Photoshop maps and connect them to the shader, which is finally assigned to the model."

Figure 7.7: How could you not love this critter?

Figure 7.8: Orodromeus leg skinnings

Meteor's texture artists take great care to finesse the cracks, bumps, and ripples. These are created by shading gray tones. "A black line on a 50% gray background will create a wrinkle," Christine says. "A white dot will create a bump. Combining the range of gray tones from black to white, we can get those subtle details such as scar, folds, scales, and bumpy patterns." (Figure 7.9 shows a set of Orodromeus leg bump maps.) The end result of those grayscales puts the equivalent of a topographic map beneath the color map.

The texture artists use a clever technique to speed the process of wrapping the model with unique skin from side to side. "To save time, we first do it symmetrically," Christine explains. "The same textures are applied to both sides. Once we are satisfied with the result, we can tweak some details on the maps to make it look unsymmetrical and more natural."

The Orodromeus consists of three sets of unfolded UVs: body, legs, and head (see Figure 7.10). Specific textures were painted for each set (color, bump, spec, and so on). "You can notice that UVs for

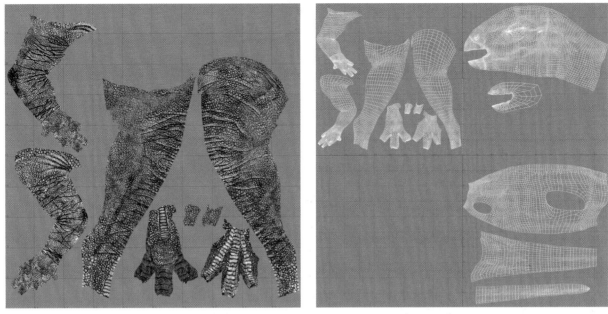

Figure 7.9: Orodromeus leg bump maps   Figure 7.10: Orodromeus layout

the head take proportionally more space than the others," explains Christine. "That allows higher resolution in textures for the head so that close-up shots look better." And you thought the Hollywood stars and starlets had the market cornered on vanity … even dinosaurs want to look good in the close-up!

Character setup is checked carefully. Christine explains how they determine whether a texture will hold up to distention and the deformation of muscles: "Deformations of muscles mean deformations of the textures. We have to take into account the way the model will deform in extreme poses and make sure that the textures don't stretch too much in those extreme postures."

Lighting is another huge consideration—it's important to ascertain whether a texture is too light or too dark. Throughout the texturing process, the team renders frequently when they create and apply the textures to the model. This allows the artists to quickly check the result to calibrate and balance the contrasts of the color, as well as the bump maps and other attributes. "For rendering, we use a basic and neutral pre-light setup that represents the values and intensities of the lights in the real scene," she says. "This process guarantees a balance that will be refined in the final shot by the lighters." Figure 7.11 shows the Orodromeus in a final render.

A Visual Effects Society Visual Effects Awards 2003 Nominee!

Meteor Studios was recognized by the Visual Effects Society for their exceptional visual effects and matte painting efforts on Dinosaur Planet. Sebastien Dostie, Claude Precourt, and Isabelle Riva were nominated for *Outstanding Visual Effects in a Television Miniseries, Movie or a Special.* Arnaud Brisebois, Philippe Roberge, and Sean Samuels were nominated for *Outstanding Matte Painting in a Televised Program, Music Video or Commercial.*

Figure 7.11: An Orodromeus, home on the range

On Photoshop and Maya

Christine is a veteran Photoshopper: "I've been using Photoshop for more then ten years. Before working in the 3D business, I was working as a designer, and we've always used Photoshop for a broad range of tasks, from boards of presentation to graphic design." These days, Christine spends a considerable amount of time in Photoshop. "Since I'm working in 3D as a texture artist, I would say that half my time is spent in Photoshop, drawing a texture with a graphic tablet and testing it after in Maya. It's a constant back and forth." Through it all, Christine declares Photoshop "an indispensable tool for every 2D and 3D artist."

Christine learned 3D with Alias Power Animator, in 1997. From there, she found the process of learning Maya to be fairly easy. "The most difficult thing was to get familiar with the new windows and menus," Christine says. "I would say that the first 3D software you learn is the toughest because you have to understand the whole 3D world." Making the leap to the next application is simplified once you master the principles. "From one software to the other, it is more a matter of being familiar with the different tools. It is important to get a general overview of the entire software that you use, a basic knowledge of every module: animation, rendering, modeling, and so on. That way you are able to understand the philosophy behind the tools and therefore to be efficient working with them."

Company Bio: Meteor's Rise

Company Meteor Studios

Location Montreal, Quebec, Canada

Website: www.meteorstudios.com/

Staff More than 120 employees

Founded 2001

Meteor was founded by Pierre de Lespinois in January 2001, with backing from Evergreen Films (where de Lespinois is president and CEO) and the Discovery Channel. The studio began production of *When Dinosaurs Roamed America* for the Discovery Channel that summer, ramping up from a staff of three to a full-scale production house status in a mere six months. Their rise, dare we say it, was meteoric. The company now employs approximately 120 and hosts 65 Maya workstations and a massive 400-processor render farm.

Meteor's expertise centers on three distinct areas: incredibly realistic creatures, engineering marvels, and atmospheric effects. Many of their pieces have been recognized with industry awards and nominations. Meteor's first effort, *When Dinosaurs Roamed America,* won the 2002 International Monitor Award for Best 3D Animation in a Television Special and was a 2002 Primetime Emmy nominee for Outstanding Television Special. Their work on *James Cameron's Expedition Bismarck* was rewarded with a 2002 Visual Effects Society Award nomination for Best Visual Effects in a Television Special. The studio's *Weather Extreme* won the 2002 International Monitor Award for Best Visual Effects in a Television Special.

eight

The New Tradition—Adding 3D to Graphic Illustrations

For more than a decade, *Michael Elins has blended*
the worlds of traditional photography and illustration to great acclaim. In
2003, Michael began to expand the scope of his work to include elements
rendered in Maya and composited in Photoshop. His groundbreaking
hybrid artwork has graced the pages of Time, Vanity Fair, *and the* New
York Times Sunday Magazine, *among others.*

Classical Beginnings

Michael attended the American Academy of Art in Chicago, which he deems a traditional
school in terms of classical painting and drawing. His first professional goal was to be an
illustrator. Upon graduation, Michael worked at a large art studio in Chicago, with more
than 100 people on staff. The studio's forte was commercial art and production, including
the (now) arcane arts of keylining and pasteup. The shop maintained a staff of specialists,
including illustrators, retouchers, designers, and lettering artists.

Those early days were very different from now. "There was no crossover, back then.
Designers designed, illustrators illustrated, retouchers retouched, and production artists only
did production," says Michael. "It's interesting how this new world has blown away those
old barriers." At some point, Michael became entranced with movie poster art. "When I was
in school, one of my goals was to simply have an office with a movie poster on the wall,"
Michael admits. Little did he know that one day he would produce movie posters for the
biggest studios in Hollywood. The way in which it happened was right out of a movie script.
Michael sought out a famous illustrator he admired in California. When they met, the illus-
trator encouraged Michael to move from Chicago to Los Angeles. Michael began working as
a freelance illustrator in the world of movie poster art in the mid 1980s.

From the mid 1980s until the early 1990s Michael was a successful freelance illustrator. In 1992, Michael hooked up with an illustration mentor who had started an annex to his
Chicago digital art studio in LA. The studio was built around a Quantel Graphic Paintbox.

The Quantel Paintbox was a groundbreaking device in its time. Michael came into the world of computer graphics cold. At the time he joined the studio, Michael had zero knowledge of computer graphics or computers in general. Things quickly changed. As he mastered Paintbox, Michael began to help run the company.

He began working on projects with famous photographers, handling some of the digital retouching chores. He did a considerable amount of work on the photographs, sometimes going way beyond simple retouching. His fame grew as the clients saw what Michael could do by mixing painting with photography. Then, in 1999, when Elizabeth Stewart, a fashion editor from the *New York Times* called to brainstorm about a project, Michael asked, "Who's shooting?" When Elizabeth replied, "You're shooting it," Michael's career took another big turn. From that project onward, Michael has shot all his own work.

After becoming familiar with Quantel Paintbox, the Macintosh was easy to pick up, and Michael soon became a Photoshop power user. The switch to a more open platform was a boon. While early on, the Paintbox provided many more options, it ran on a dedicated platform and was a hardware-intensive machine. The Mac changed the world, and Michael's fame began to soar.

Maya was added to the mix in early 2003, to great effect.

Bio: Michael Elins

Michael Elins is a renowned Southern California–based photographer and illustrator. After years of working in traditional media, Michael now ranks as a Photoshop power user and has been incorporating 3D into his illustrations with the help of Maya artists since 2003. Michael's work has appeared in *Time*, the *New York Times*, *Newsweek*, and other high-profile publications. See more of his work at **www.michaelelins.com**.

The Alanis Morissette Project

Michael's journey into the world of Maya began when the *New York Times* came to him with a project for the Style section. The project, featuring best-selling singer-songwriter Alanis Morissette, is noteworthy because it was designed to extend from a print fashion story into a animated web project. Once the project was underway, Alanis's label, Maverick Records, asked for it to be fleshed out into a video. "I wanted to do a print project that would also go on the web," says Michael. "The idea was that the still pictures would come alive on the web." The narrative of the piece is based on a song Alanis wrote, titled "Precious Illusions." "My idea was to take advantage of the web, in a way that most print publications neglect to do," he continues. "Typically the magazines upload their still pictures to the web. But my thinking was, 'As long as it's on the web, it should move. As long as it's on the web and it's Alanis, you should hear the song.'"

Michael went back to his original notebook. "These projects come from the inside out," he explains. "My thinking is done in the beginning, and the execution comes from the thinking, not the other way around." Michael decided to go the 3D route early on, using Maya for modeling and animation. This was the first time that Michael had ever worked with a 3D artist. At the time, he was working with producer Bob Self. "I sat down with Bob and said, 'I have these ideas,' and we started talking about it," Michael explains. "Bob helped me turn them into a reality. For all intents and purposes, he was the visual coordinator. I gave him the pictures and elements, and he assembled and edited the piece." It was Bob who introduced Michael to 3D and the Gnomon School of Visual Effects–trained 3D artist Linas Jodwallis. "Hooking up with Michael was random," says Linas. "I was in a miniaturist class at Gnomon. Bob Self, one of my classmates, turned out to be a friend of Michael's." At the time, Bob and Michael were already at work on the Alanis project. One thing lead to another, and Linas soon signed on for his first paid 3D gig.

The work was largely created in Adobe After Effects. They used Maya to build two environments within the Alanis piece: the billboard and the freeway. In Figure 8.1a, the billboard is shown from behind when it first fades into view. The camera pans in tight on the backward C in COMPLETE and tracks across the word, from right to left. As the scene begins, it's not obvious that this is a billboard. The view quickly pulls away and to the right to reveal the entire billboard in shadow, against a fiery red sky (see Figure 8.2b).

The camera continues to move as it rotates around and away from the billboard (see Figures 8.2a and 8.2b). As the camera moves away and to the front, the billboard becomes more obvious.

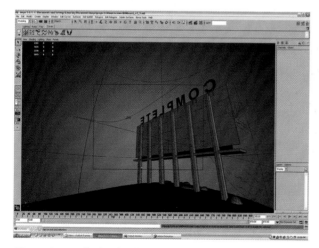

Figure 8.1a: The back of the billboard in wireframe

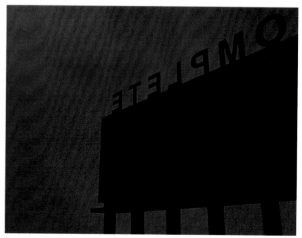

Figure 8.1b: The back of the billboard rendered

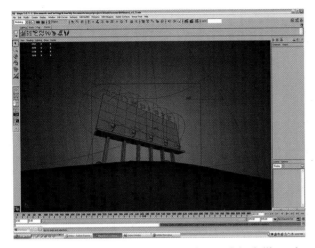

Figure 8.2a: Spinning around to the front of the billboard in wireframe

Figure 8.2b: The front of the billboard rendered

Figure 8.3: The lighted billboard

Figure 8.4: Driving down the freeway

Spotlights sputter on to illuminate images of Alanis on the face of the billboard (see Figure 8.3) with light. The images shuffle like puzzle pieces as the camera zooms into a single image of Alanis that continues a rapid puzzle shuffle.

Although the billboard is more introductory in nature, the freeway is central to the piece. The freeway is shown during daylight and at night. At times the freeway is shot from below, from afar, and ultimately above. Within the storyline, the camera cuts back and forth to the freeway, from the vantage point of being in a car on the freeway, with road signs. The scenes shot on the freeway impart an unmistakable feeling of motion, with a surrealistic video-game–like quality (see Figure 8.4)

At the end of the video, the camera pulls back (see Figures 8.5a and 8.5b) to reveal that we have been driving within letterforms, in the shape of two words. The ribbon of highway becomes the words *so long*.

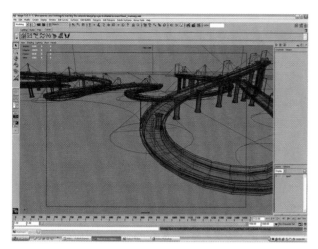

Figure 8.5a: The camera begins to pull back in wireframe

Figure 8.5b: The camera pulling back, rendered

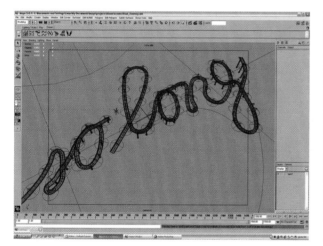

Figure 8.6a: The words revealed in Maya

Figure 8.6b: The final words rendered

Viewed from high above, the freeway almost appears to be a slot car track. Figures 8.6a and 8.6b show the words/freeway from a lofty vantage point. "You could never have a crane that big," Michael exclaims.

"It's the idea of an extended storyboard," Michael explains. "Whereas previously a photographer or illustrator would be doing a still photograph or illustration, now it's possible to extend a concept almost indefinitely with the tools at our disposal." Although Michael does not work within Maya, he has adapted it into his workflow by working with Maya artists. "In this new paradigm, many programs make up the project," he continues. "My elements can move between print and motion worlds." The finished piece is a fine example of collaborative effort. "The video could not have been done without the significant contribution of Bob Self, who did the After Effects work," says Michael. See the final version of the movie on this book's companion CD.

The *Time* DNA Cover

In early 2003, *Time* magazine called Michael to create a cover celebrating the discovery of DNA. Being a project of such magnitude, the cover art took a significant amount of planning. "The first step in any of my projects is research. I look through my extensive collection of art books and start sketching," he explains. Reference material is of utmost importance to Michael. "I try very, very hard to be open-minded when I start a project, *not* to fit the project into a canned formula," continues Michael. "By looking at books, I am opening my mind up to all the possibilities. I look at the art for inspiration." In this case, Michael came up with the idea of DNA and creation, which led him to Adam and Eve.

Michael's perspective harks back to the Renaissance or Post-Renaissance. "When I was looking at paintings that were religious allegories, I thought that would be a perfect way to tell the DNA story from a human point of view, to treat it as an allegory, with people and symbols." Much of Michael's work revolves around his interest in the human form. He eventually came up with the idea of a naked Adam and Eve, holding hands, wrapped in a golden strand of DNA, which morphs upward into a tree. Michael did some pencil sketches and e-mailed scans of the initial sketches to *Time* magazine in New York City (see Figure 8.7).

The time frames on Michael's projects are most often very tight. He typically gets an initial call on Tuesday afternoon or Wednesday morning, with the final project due in New York City by Friday evening. After getting a go-ahead on the pencil sketches, Michael called his photography producer, John Collazos, who helped put the preproduction schedule together for the photo shoot. This entails hiring models and assistants and booking a studio. The producer sent a call to the modeling agency, which sent a stack of cards that were quickly whittled down to ten models. Michael then photographed the tree on the streets of Palisades Park on 2¼-inch medium-format film (see Figure 8.8).

At this point, Maya was brought into the mix. Michael called Linas Jodwallis, and explained what pieces he needed and

Figure 8.7: The original pencil-on-graphite sketch of Adam and Eve

Figure 8.8: The trees were shot conventionally, with the resulting transparency drum-scanned.

Figure 8.9: The surreal sky is a result of much interplay between Maya and Photoshop, not to mention many layers.

Figure 8.10: The models in their natural state, with their private parts covered, for newsstand considerations

his vision for the piece. Michael e-mailed the pencil sketch scan, and Linas began his work in Maya by producing a fabulous synthetic sky background image. Linas built the sky from scratch, starting with textures created in Maya.

Linas made great use of Maya's Paint Effects and Fluids to build the clouds and spent a good bit of time moving between Maya and Photoshop. "I took pieces in Maya and rendered out some clouds that I could use sections [of]," Linas explains. "Then, I combined that with other sections in Photoshop, brought that back into Maya, rendered it onto a sphere, made it a hemispherical texture, and wrapped it onto another sphere." Once that was complete, Linas finished things off, as he added in more fluids with fog and blended the color upward from the horizon (see Figure 8.9).

As Linas worked on the background image and double helix, Michael was in the studio, doing the photo shoot, where capturing the moment has proven to be at the core of his success.

"Photography is intimate and immediate and very much about connecting with the soul of the subject," he explains. "Every picture is different. Being a photographer is a unique experience; it's not like being a painter." The result of the photo session, as shown in Figure 8.10, is an image of the models with their souls laid bare (along with the majority of their skin). As famed photographer Henri Cartier-Bresson (born 1908) put it, a photographer must align his brain, eye, and heart. Like Michael, Cartier-Bresson was a painter before he took up the camera.

Once the photo shoot was completed, Michael moved onto the next phase, in which he literally paints his photographs. As he does, Michael brings with him the essence of the shoot. "It's an intangible," he reveals. "You draw on the experience that you had with these people; it's a mini-relationship. You take that with you when you work on the painting in Photoshop." From the raw photographs, Michael seeks a more perfect human form, one that is free of blemishes and imperfections.

Figure 8.11: The double helix replete with reflections

With the photography and paint-over work done, Linas was able to finish work on the double helix and to map the image of the models to the double helix. Linas freely admits that "it took a while to model the helix, because I'm not a math guy." He took the photograph and made rough objects that looked like human silhouettes. Then he projected the photographs onto the objects. "When I was raytracing, ready to render, I turned off the visibility of the objects, but left all the reflections and refractions," he explains. "It ended up looking great, although it wasn't mathematically correct." The end result of the modeling and rendering is shown in Figure 8.11.

At this point, with all the elements complete, Michael began composting the four separate files in Photoshop. Michael views his role as the director of the project, with all the 3D elements created to live in the piece. The sky and double helix produced in Maya were adjusted to fit with the other elements in the picture. Michael spends a good bit of time adjusting the color and contrast. "To make all the elements come together in the picture is when I draw upon my time spent painting," he explains. "You need to understand color theory. It took me a while to understand color theory back when I was in art school. Once you get it, it's basic." When painting a color from scratch, mixing colors together, you're creating from your brain. Bringing in disparate pieces is a different situation. "When I have elements from different sources, such as photos and 3D pieces, it all has to work together in the final scene."

The secret to life, it's said, is to love what you do for a living. "What's so much fun about doing these projects is that you get to experience the different crafts," Michael says. "The most important part of this is that you enjoy the process … the concept, the sketching, the photography, the 3D work in Maya, the Photoshop work…." It is integral, he believes, to respect and enjoy the process, as you will always be in one step or another at any given time.

Michael's creative process is filled with questions and doubts along the way. "It's hard to be objective when you are in the midst of the process," explains Michael. "At any given time when you work with one of these publications, you have no idea if your work will be used or not." Without an indication of whether your work will be recognized, Michael continues, "the only way to not go crazy and to be effective at what you are doing is to focus exclusively on the project." He freely admits to thinking about the work at night and dreaming about the projects. "I try to just think about the project I am working on. There are always bigger things, but I have found that focusing on the process is the best way to get things done," he says. "When I was much younger, I would think naively that it would immediately make a difference in the world. But it's just a process, like laying brick. Eventually, you have a wall." The project was completed—wire to wire—in four days. With deadlines this tight, Michael will shoot off low-resolution JPEG images to the magazine for the approval process and so that the layout artists can begin working on the cover. "Working with the news magazines is liquid," Michael explains. "It's a matter of working quickly and being able to respond to the comments and make adjustments." Figure 8.12 shows the final image.

Generally speaking, Michael works at "rez 24," with enough image to yield an 8-x-10-inch transparency. As a result, his Photoshop files are huge. This practice is a holdover from his movie poster work. A 70MB flattened Photoshop file can be blown up and used as movie poster art. And it's plenty big for the cover of *Time*.

Figure 8.12:
Time *magazine,
February 17,
2003. Compare
the final image
against the origi-
nal photograph.*

Little Blue Pills

Time magazine came to Michael again in early 2004 to create a piece on the crossing of the threshold between natural human biology and medical technology in the area of sexual health. This piece was slated to run in *Time*'s annual health and medicine issue to illustrate an article about the advent of drugs such as Viagra and Premarin. Once again, Michael collaborated with Maya artist Linas Jodwallis, to use cutting-edge techniques to create a stunning piece of editorial artwork with a classical feel. The original concept sketch is shown in Figure 8.13.

The dry, parched desert provides a stark yet beautiful backdrop (see Figure 8.14). Linas created the desert using a toned-down Fluid lake in Maya. The lake was textured with photographic images and tweaked in Photoshop. Linas uses a huge library of photography that he's shot himself. "Buying someone else's textures? That's no fun!" he states, "I take high-res photographs of everything: textures, rocks, concrete, bricks, floor tiles, glass, ground, landscapes, metals, skins, and stucco. I could never make anything photoreal without real photographic textures." A couple of Photographic texturing classes in Maya helped Linas learn the ropes. The sky was created in a manner similar to that in the DNA artwork, using a layer-upon-layer technique.

Michael shot the doorway in the studio digitally. Little blue lights run on the ground toward the doorway and then up and around the door frame. The door ajar creates an air of expectation. The doorway was shot twice, once with strobe lighting (see Figure 8.15a) and once without (see Figure 8.15b). "If you put strobes in a room, they will overwhelm the ambient light," Michael illuminates. "To see the Christmas lights, you have to turn off the strobes." The two exposures were then layered in Photoshop using a layer-masking

Figure 8.13: The original sketch

Figure 8.14: The desert background, as created in Maya

Figure 8.15a: The doorway strobed   *Figure 8.15b: The doorway unstrobed*

technique, with just the lights painted in. The result was a bright room with glowing Christmas lights.

Michael's work relies on both allegory and symbolism. "These new drugs seemed as if they would apply to a surrealistic world," Michael explains. "It made me think of the surrealists that I admire. With Salvador Dali, for example, you would have a melting clock in the desert." With that in mind, the allegory of the doorway represents the threshold. With symbolism, an element means something different to each person.

But it is the human element that is the most important. Michael's elegant lighting of the human form brings the piece to a classical level. "I wanted the piece to be simple in terms of lighting with the classical effect of one light source and reflected light," he explains. "The poses are meant to be reminiscent of a religious allegory from the Renaissance." The unretouched studio shots are shown in Figure 8.16.

The lyre, or brass scrollwork, that surrounds the doorway might be thought of as a visual prompt to the brass bed. But it goes a good bit deeper than that. One only need look back to ancient Greece to learn that the lyre was an attribute of the Greek god of love, Eros. Linas created the scrollwork in Maya, and the shadows were cast on the desert floor. The lyre is shown in Figure 8.17.

Figure 8.16: Classical beauty

Figure 8.17: And you wondered how the lyre became part of the bed frame?

The montage of medical supplies was created from studio shots and supplied images. In this project, Michael shot completely digitally, using an eleven megapixel Canon D1S camera. The work was challenging, in that it was a highly complicated piece, yet it needed to be done in just a few days. Figure 8.18 shows the finished piece.

As things turned out, this piece did not run in *Time* magazine's annual health and medicine issue. "It's always a chance you take," Michael explains. "And with the news magazines, it's a bigger chance. It can happen any time you work editorially—you can get bumped at any moment by another story."

Figure 8.18: The finished piece

Giants of Media

In early 2004, *Newsweek* magazine asked Michael to create an illustration to portray the war between the giants of satellite, cable, and content media. The initial direction from *Newsweek* was that the image should look like the scene from the classic 1933 film, *King Kong. Newsweek* asked that the titans of industry appear in a King Kong-ish manner, towering over the city, while swarmed with aircraft. The discussion took a turn when Michael posed the question, What's King Kong standing on? Michael recalled that in the famous shot from the original film, King Kong was in fact, standing on the Empire State Building's spire, not on a flat rooftop. (The folks at *Newsweek* may initially have been thinking of the 1976 Dino De Laurentiis remake, in which Kong fends off the airplanes while straddling the roofs of the World Trade Center's twin towers.)

In initial discussions, Michael determined that the image would need four or five spires. He thought this would look odd, not to mention being difficult to source, as a picture of each spire. It quickly became clear that architectural photographs wouldn't work for this project. "We would not have sufficient resolution in a photograph," Michael explains. "And just as important, the odds of the buildings being at the right angle would be a trillion to one." He needed buildings in the exact position to shoot the body doubles.

The project team went back and forth over the details. Finally, Michael realized that he would have to ditch the spires and go with spireless buildings instead. *Newsweek* agreed to have the media magnets stand on top of the buildings once the production difficulties were explained. Michael sketched out the conceptual rough shown in Figure 8.19. With that battle won, Michael still needed a suitable cityscape to work with. Photo archives didn't provide the answer. Maya did.

Michael hooked up with Marc-André Guindon, a Montreal-based Maya expert. "I sent Marc a composite of the piece without the buildings, and he built them at the exact angles and perspectives, with the right coloring and textures," explains Michael. With a tight deadline, Marc made quick work of the Empire State Building. Figure 8.20 shows a wireframe of the top of the building.

Figure 8.19: The giants of media rough

Even with the tight deadline, the building was meticulously textured. When the texturing was complete, Marc placed a skyline photo of Manhattan behind the building and began lighting the image. A test render is shown in Figure 8.21.

When all was well, Marc made final renders and shipped them to Michael. "All I had to do when I got the finished buildings was do some color correction and pop them into my Photoshop piece, and it was out the door." Of course, it's not always quite *that* easy. The client ultimately made several changes, which required Marc to go back and alter some of the architecture. Figure 8.22 shows the positioning of the buildings within Maya, and Figure 8.23 shows the final composite of the first iteration.

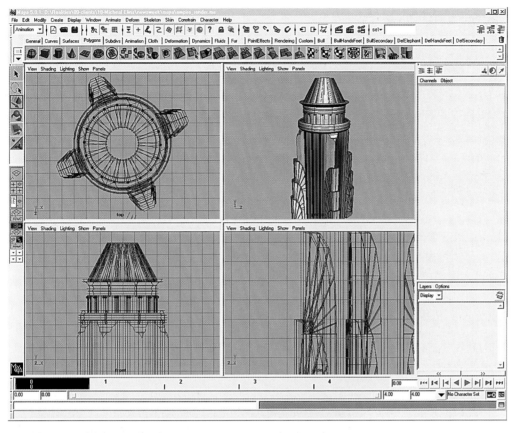

Figure 8.20: The top of the Empire State Building in wireframe

Figure 8.21: Five points for each building you can name in the background

Figure 8.22: Posing the Giants of Media

Figure 8.23: Rupert Murdoch fends off the airplanes with a satellite dish.

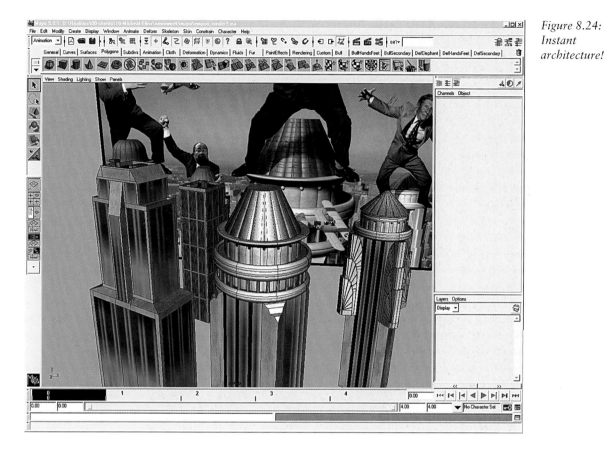

Figure 8.24: Instant architecture!

The project originally started, at the client's request, with four Empire State Building tops. Once the final composite was finished, *Newsweek* decided they didn't want all four buildings to be similar. This put Michael and Marc into overdrive to complete the extensive changes in architecture in order to meet deadline. "I had to fit the remodeling into my schedule," explains Marc. "I quickly made changes to the models, put on the textures and details, and shipped it." As soon as Marc got the buildings done, it was approved.

The extensive changes to the buildings were done quickly. "We could have put more effort into it to make it a more awesome image," Marc explains. "But we were stuck giving the client images very quickly." To come up with four distinct buildings, Marc altered one of the Empire State Buildings to create two new structures and built the fourth building from scratch. Figure 8.24 shows the revised set of buildings as they are being positioned within Maya

"In this process, nothing is linear," says Michael. "It is never step 1, step 2, step 3, step 4 ... there is always the human factor." Figure 8.25 shows the final poses of: Rupert Murdoch, chairman and chief executive of the News Corporation Ltd., which owns Fox; Richard Parsons, chairman and CEO of Time Warner Inc.; Sumner M. Redstone of Viacom International Inc.; and Brian L. Roberts, president and CEO of Comcast Corp.

The editorial gremlins struck once again. After the intense work to get the piece finished, it was bumped by the Martha Stewart trial.

Figure 8.25: The giants of media: Murdoch, Parsons, Redstone, and Roberts

Maya in Perspective

Michael sees it all from an art history perspective. "From an artistic standpoint, when any kind of new technology is introduced, the first application our small human brains can figure out is to put them to a task that we used the old technology for," he explains. "The first thing we thought of was retouching. Then we thought of compositing. In these first few years of digital artwork, we have been basically getting rid of all the obvious, all the stuff you would expect people to do. What is starting to happen now is that we are beginning to push the boundaries and add to the timeline of art history."

Re-creating existing media isn't what fuels Michael's fire. "In the early software packages, people would say, 'Wouldn't it be nice to do a watercolor painting on a computer?' That is a totally useless thing to do," he exhorts. "The history and merging of medium and styles is allowing us to open doors to new kinds of projects that we could never imagine when we first started with this new technology."

"The reason that this is so organized in my head," Michael explains, "is that this is a complete accident of timing." Having spent so much time drawing and painting, with no other aspirations, Michael learned how to conceptualize and how to bring the vision in his head through his hands to the canvas. "I killed myself to become the best painter I could be," he freely admits. What Michael didn't realize was that the time he spent drawing and painting pictures would pay off in spades in the new medium. "While there are big fat manuals for software programs, think of the amount of time that it takes to learn how to draw and paint as a professional illustrator," he explains. "It takes so much brush mileage and thought, and there are no shortcuts." Michael feels lucky, for when he stopped painting and dived into the digital arts studio, he had no idea that all that brush mileage would lead to such success in the new medium.

"There's a process when you do this kind of work—the concept and the execution, and generally we talk about the execution—you did this in Photoshop and that in Maya," explains Michael. "In the beginning you need your own thesis, your own take on the subject."

nine

Re-creating Egyptian Antiquities

Take a trip *to www.EternalEgypt.org, and you'll travel back in time*
... a trip made possible with Maya and Photoshop. The voyage was piloted by designers at IBM's e-business Innovation Center who wielded a cutting-edge mix of tools to re-create Egyptian architecture and artifacts in a complex interactive installation for the Egyptian Museum in Cairo, Egypt. Their project includes digital re-creations of King Tutankhamun's tomb, the temple at Luxor, the Giza plateau and Great Pyramids, and the city of Alexandria. The idea is not just to re-create artifacts as they are now, but as they were when they were first built thousands of years ago.

The project uses Digital Guide–powered handheld computers within the museum, as well as a website. With a Digital Guide, a museum visitor can obtain contextual information within the museum—providing visual and written details, in addition to the spoken word. As visitors move through the museum, they have the benefit of listening to the tour narration on their headset, with in-depth information and animation available on the Digital Guide. The Digital Guides were implemented first, followed by the website in early 2004. Interactive kiosks to showcase the content at other museums around the world are scheduled to follow by the end of 2004. Made possible through a generous IBM grant to the Egyptian government, the project sets a high bar, as it takes a path that has never been followed before.

A Worldwide Effort

Led by Media Director Colin Freeman, the IBM e-business Innovation Center's 3D develop-ment team consists of four 3D developers, a creative director, two project managers, numer-ous Flash developers, one Shockwave programmer, and several other technicians. The team uses real-time robotic cameras, 3D scanners, and other IBM hardware. Although Maya and Photoshop were the two primary software workhorses, the Interactive Media team also used DeepPaint 3D, Curious Labs Poser, REALVIZ Stitcher (for stitching together panoramic images), and Hash's Animation Master (for some of the modeling). The Interactive Media team began the extensive project in 2002. In addition to team members on site in Egypt, the effort was mostly spread out across the United States, with developers in Atlanta, Boston, and California, as well as in Canada.

Figure 9.1: The Sphinx shown in its original and present states, in QTVR view

The project uses linked QuickTimeVR (QTVR) movies to help the museum visitor become immersed in the digital environment. "Let's say I want to see the Giza plateau," explains Colin. "I'll click a point on the map, which will open a QuickTimeVR file. Then, I'll click a hotspot in the QuickTimeVR movie, and the camera will move to the new location and load a new movie." This technique provides a compelling view into the ancient world, as well as into its present state (see Figure 9.1).

The flybys are displayed at www.eternalegypt.org (see Figure 9.1a) in a QuickTime format, wrapped in Shockwave. The group produced many interactive QTVRs, which have been networked together with animation in-betweens to create virtual walkthroughs.

The www.eternalegypt.com website allows folks to visit sites such as the Giza plateau (see Figure 9.1b), without booking a flight overseas. A cross-section of one of the Great Pyramids (see Figure 9.1c) provides a unique look into the ancient construction technique.

The Sphinx is one of Egypt's most familiar landmarks. The website's QTVR representations of the original (see Figure 9.1d) and current (see Figure 9.1e) states of the Sphinx show the dramatic changes over time. Erosion from centuries of natural sandblasting has worn away the original surface and coloring.

The group aims to use Shockwave as an envelope for file formats including QTVR and Flash. A 400-×-400-pixel universal GUI acts as the container.

Figure 9.1a: The companion website www.eternalegypt.org

Figure 9.1b: The Giza plateau at **www.eternalegypt.org**

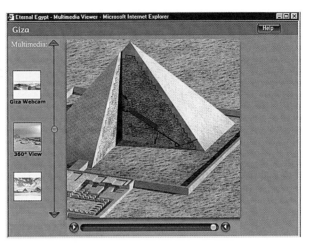

Figure 9.1c: A pyramid cross-section at **www.eternalegypt.org**

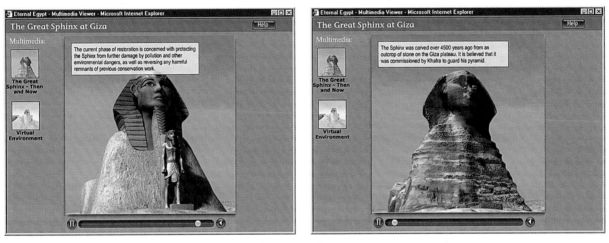

Figure 9.1d and Figure 9.1e: A QTVR shows the Sphinx through the ages at **www.eternalegypt.org.**

Modeling and Texturing

The largest models are extensive, with polygon counts ranging in the six figures and upward. Although the team developed a number of models from scratch, the project purchased other models. The meshes and textures for the city of Alexandria, while obtained from an outside source, were extensively modified to meet the level of detail necessary in the project.

Here's a tally on some of the largest polygon counts:

- Luxor: 4 × 400,000
- Tutankhamun's Tomb: 1 × 400,000
- City of Alexandria: more than 1,000,000
- Giza plateau (see Figure 9.2): more than 400,000 and growing (may total more than 500,000 upon completion)

Figure 9.2: The Giza plateau

Modeling the Giza Plateau

Because of the immense scale of the environment, modeling the terrain proved to be a considerable challenge, particularly in the Giza plateau. "In any 3D model you have a world that has a certain amount of space," explains Colin. "And then there are all the objects that need to fit into that space." Although Maya allows for shadow maps to save time in rendering, the Giza files proved to be too large in scale to follow that methodology. "The Giza plateau files were packed with 4000-×-4000-pixel shadow maps," Colin continues. "If a pyramid was 400 meters wide, the end result showed just a 4-pixel shadow width, so I had to raytrace instead."

The team strove for an accurate representation of the terrain, relying primarily on satellite maps and other supporting material. "You look at a satellite map, and it's straight down," Colin explains. "This provides a good start for reference material, but you can't always see certain details. You have to look closely at the shadows." Although the team did not have access to survey data, they were able to use some rough topographic maps as reference.

Although accuracy was a primary goal, so too was functionality in the final delivery. The environments could not be too complex to play on lesser devices. To this end, the team made decisions to limit complexity on the largest areas. "I set up a flat plain in Maya and started roughing it out with polygonal areas," Colin explains. "Then I drew out the rough map of the plateau and had to pick areas that were flat and leave them as flat polygons. The mesh was then subdivided in order to get it all to work." In highly detailed areas, the team used the Sculpt Polygon tool, a Paintbrush that allows the artist to sculpt as if with clay. The result is a terrain that provides an acceptable level of detail without being a million-polygon mesh.

Modeling the Giza plateau was an iterative process. "I had to remodel Giza three times or so," Colin says. "The first time it didn't work. The second time it was closer, but just not close enough. So I reworked it again to add details like the quarry lines." As the team got deeper into the project, more information came to light. This was the case with the area where the blocks were quarried for the pyramids.

Texturing proved to be a substantial endeavor, as well. The group found that, because of the scale of the models and the variability in camera position, one texture might not cover all the bases for any given object. Texturing depends on the distance of the camera from the object. The pyramids provide a good example of the quandary. "We used a pyramid block photo for the color and then used a noise channel for the bump map," Colin explains. "This works well up close, but when you zoom out, the noise begins to look too even. We have to play around with the randomness of the noise attributes, based on the camera position." To ease the dilemma, Colin has considered writing a MEL script to handle the variability in textures, based on distance from the camera.

Blurring the Lines

The Giza plateau's terrain image maps are a beefy 4000 × 4000 pixels. To avoid pixelization at eye level, the team used Maya shaders to fractalize bumps, creating seamless bump maps to simulate rocks and pebbles. They also made great use of Photoshop's Gaussian Blur filter to reduce high-contrast levels.

As Colin explains, Giza is an atmospheric place, with lots of fog and haze. As you'll see later in this chapter, the team used a bloom effect to help create the atmosphere that was absent in the original renders. In addition, Photoshop was used to add sun and lens flares to the QTVRs.

Reconstructing King Tutankhamun's Tomb

King Tutankhamun, the most famous—and reportedly the youngest—of all Egyptian kings, ascended the throne as a child and died while still a teenager. Tut's post-mortem fame grew, not necessarily because of his prominence as a ruler, but because of the discovery of his untouched tomb by British archeologist Howard Carter in the early 1920s. Although grave robbers plundered tombs of other Egyptian kings, King Tut's tomb was spared. Figure 9.3 shows a view of Tut's sarcophagus as it would have been placed.

Of the many treasures found in King Tutankhamun's tomb, the Canopic Shrine of Tutankhamun and the Funerary Mask of Tutankhamun are among the most famous.

The Canopic Shrine of Tutankhamun

As was the common practice of the day, Tut's mummification process was extensive. The Canopic Shrine of Tutankhamun contains the vital organs that were removed from the mummy—including the brain, kidney, and liver—in four separate canopic coffins. The four

Figure 9.3: King Tutankhamun's tomb in its original state

Figure 9.4: The Canopic Shrine of Tutankhamun

vessels were housed inside a shrine of quartzite and placed on a sled. The shrine of quartzite was surrounded by an ornate gilded wooden shrine, which was placed on another sled. Four protective goddesses—Neith, Selkis, Isis, and Nephthys—guard the outer shrine (see Figure 9.4).

The team modeled everything in King Tut's tomb from scratch, including the canopic shrine. Although the team found a low-resolution virtual reality model on the Web to use as a reference for the tomb, it merely provided a starting point to re-create the environment in Maya.

Visit www.EternalEgypt.org to see an exploded view of the Canopic Shrine of Tutankhamun. The exploded view reveals the inner quartzitic shrine. The alabaster stoppers, each in the form of Tutankhamun's head, are visible atop the individual canopic coffins. The smaller sled is visible, as well. Through the magic of Maya, and the hard work of the IBM e-business Innovation Center team, museum visitors can explore the Canopic Shrine as never before.

The Funerary Mask of Tutankhamun

The ancient Egyptians used funerary masks to cover and protect the mummy's face. None is so well known as the solid gold funerary mask of King Tutankhamun. The mask was placed over the head of the mummy, inside the inner sarcophagus. Ornate details, including the vulture and cobra on the headdress and false beard of divinity, befit the young king. "Building these objects in Maya gives you an appreciation for what the artists did back then," says Colin. "I can't imagine the time that went into the building of the funeral masks." Inlaid stones included lapis lazuli and quartz (see Figure 9.5).

Although there was a good bit of reference material, texturing the ornate funerary mask of King Tutankhamun was a challenge. The funerary mask was recast as it was found, after a bit of cleanup. "There are small blemishes here and there," Colin explains. "But the computer version looks a little more pristine than the original, particularly with regard to the areas on the original where garnets have fallen off." The intent of the project was to show the whole tomb as it was found by Carter. After producing a pristine model of the funerary mask, the team used grunge maps to make the model look more like the condition in which it was found.

When taking a normal 3D production from scratch to photo-realistic stage, most artists travel through the steps of modeling, lighting, texturing, and rendering. They then tweak things and travel back into Photoshop to make it all look as photo-realistic as possible. "We had lots of time to spend on modeling and spent the majority of time there,

Figure 9.5: The Funerary Mask of Tutankhamun, re-created in Maya

Figure 9.6: King Tutankhamun's Funerary Mask, shown in a Maya montage

followed by texturing," Colin explains. "We didn't have as much time in lighting and rendering as we would have liked. Grunge maps and specular maps make the renders look so much more realistic." From the front, the wireframe view of the Funerary Mask of Tutankhamun shows the highly realistic facial details.

When you view the mask from multiple angles, without the stone inlays, you gain a huge appreciation for the amount of work it took to forge the solid gold funerary mask. Figure 9.6 provides an interesting look into the process. "This rendering was just something that I did for myself," says Colin. "I was doing some experiments with radiosity rendering and wanted to create a progression of a model from wireframe to shaded version to rendered version." A bit of work was done in Photoshop to clean things up.

Along with Colin, the Maya team included William Victor and Brett Gardy. Colin, William, and Brett worked hard to provide as much realism as possible, within deadline constraints. "I found myself wishing for more time to make it as photo-realistic as possible," Colin explains. "I wanted to make these pieces look real, as they existed then. I didn't want people to think of them as a 3D representation. I wanted them to think that's what the pieces looked like." On deadline, the team had to make conscious decisions, which often involved weighing the question, Should I take the time modeling this, or should I fix it in Photoshop after the fact? In all, the process can be thought of as being akin to building a Hollywood set. From one angle the set looks real, but from another, it looks flat.

As beautiful as they are, both the Canopic Shrine and the Funerary Mask are among the earliest and least intricate of the 3D models produced by the IBM team with Maya and Photoshop. In the next section on Luxor, you'll see how, as Colin puts it, "things got very complex."

The Temple of Luxor

The Temple of Luxor was central to ancient Egyptian society and is now one of the world's greatest archeological treasures. Its construction was a monumental task. "The temple itself was built over many hundreds of years," Colin explains. "It started with the sanctuary, which is at the very back of the present temple. Courtyards and halls were then added over time by different pharaohs from Amenhotep to Ramesses the Great. Finally the pylons and obelisks were built at the front and engraved with a story that Ramesses put on nearly every building he constructed."

Luxor has changed dramatically since its initial construction. Over the years, great portions of the structure rose and fell. To show the changes, the Interactive Media team re-created the temple at Luxor in four distinct time periods:

- Original state with hieroglyphics
- Roman period
- Coptic period
- Current state

The flyby changes over time from ancient Luxor (see Figures 9.7 and 9.8), through Roman and Coptic periods, and the present day. Textures morph, and structural elements change with the ages. Walls and roofs vanish, while interior columns are revealed. Entire sections of structure disappear, leaving behind only traces of their foundations.

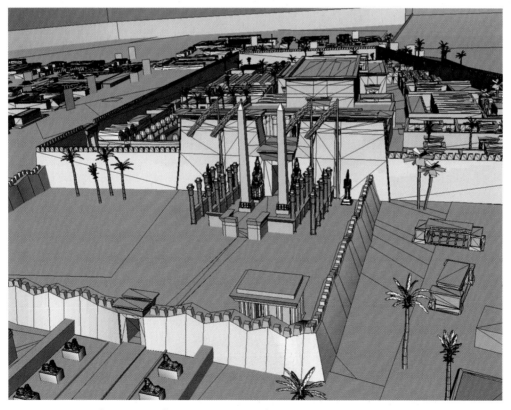

Figure 9.7: A wireframe view of Luxor in its original state

Figure 9.8 Luxor in its original state

"The temple stood for many years and was converted to a Roman fort when the Romans occupied Egypt," Colin continues. "The walls were built up... the granaries were replaced with barracks ... and several Roman temples, actually chapels, were built."

"The next time period is called Coptic, which simply means the Christian church in Egypt," explains Colin. "It's hard to see from the fly through, but several Coptic churches were built using walls of the temple and stones from the ruins of the Roman fort."

"Finally the churches became ruins and eventually the Mosque of Abul Hagaag was constructed just behind the front pylons and in the first courtyard," says Colin. "This state is the fourth and current state of the temple even though the mosque was built more than 800 years ago. We wanted to show the current state of all the objects, if we could." Figure 9.9 shows Luxor in the present day.

Figure 9.9: Luxor in its current state

The current state of Luxor was the most time-consuming to create. While the original state only had to depict the buildings with their hieroglyphs, the current state has many more structures, as well as the surrounding city and trees. And although the current state was based on structures from the earlier states, it had to use a greater variety of textures, for a more accurate portrayal. "Varying texture maps is important," explains Colin. "It's a lot harder to represent painted images on brick than it is to represent plain brick." He adds an interesting thought: "When you are re-creating a piece in a new state and it hasn't been aged, it can be harder to make it look realistic." There's something to be said for the patina of age.

On Photoshop

A veteran of the digital arts, Colin has been at the forefront of the CG world for quite some time. "I've used Photoshop since version 1, and before that, Pixel Paint Pro," he says. "I do lots of multimedia and After Effects work (production of videos and animations). Photoshop is the perfect place to start the production of my graphics."

Like many of the artists profiled in these pages, Colin finds Photoshop's layers and channels indispensable. "I use layers, obviously," Colin explains. "But more important for my use, channels allow lots of image manipulation that is much harder to do in other packages—like knocking out backgrounds in pictures."

"It is very hard to knock out backgrounds with things that are fuzzy or hairy," Colin reveals. "But I've developed some tricks with channels and with the Dodge and Burn tools that make it a snap. I also use channels to create selections of different contrasted layers of an image, for example, highlights versus shadows. This gives me all the manual control I need to manipulate images to the nth degree. To be honest... some of my tricks may even be a little outdated, but they work for me, and I haven't learned any newer or simpler way yet."

Colin also uses plug-ins such as Offset and High Pass to create seamless textures that don't have repeatable tiles. "I've just recently figured out a great way to make bump maps from color images using the High Pass and Levels filters."

The team used post effects in Photoshop to impart a higher level of realism for the QTVRs. They began by rendering the images in Maya. The rendered images were then taken into REALVIZ Stitcher to build panoramas. From there, they exported spherical maps (360° view, 3200-×-1600-pixel image) with distorted tops and bottoms. They imported the spherical maps into Photoshop to create a bloom effect. The bloom effect is meant to mimic a chemical film process in which the chemicals bleed and convey a glowing appearance to certain things.

Figures 9.10 and 9.11 show QTVR views of the Boat Museum, and Figure 9.12 shows a view from on high.

Here's Colin's recipe for the bloom effect:

- In Photoshop, duplicate the layer of an image, and erase the sky with a rough blurred brush. That will give you the ground and the horizon line.
- Overlay that image with screen or overlay or both to brighten the image.
- Do a Gaussian Blur to create a bloom effect, and crank the effect down with transparency to 50% for a screen or 20% for an overlay.
- With a transparent eraser, delete select parts of the image.

On Learning Maya

Colin came to Maya with a great deal of Photoshop experience. "I probably had seven years of Photoshop experience before I started learning Maya," he reveals. "My biggest hurdles in learning Maya were the modularity and the multiple ways to do the same thing," he continues. "These aspects confused me a little at first, but now they seem nice, and I understand when to use a technique." Colin faced a hurdle in getting used to the node-based architecture, as he was familiar with a different system. But now that he has it mastered, he enjoys getting under the hood to see what makes Maya tick.

Figure 9.10: An initial render of the Boat Museum

Figure 9.11: The final QTVR Boat Museum image

Figure 9.12: A view of Giza from atop one of the pyramids

"Modeling should be your initial step in learning Maya," says Colin. He suggests beginning with modeling polygons and then moving on to texturing. "You'll spend forever just mastering these two things," he explains. "From there you can decide if you want to learn the other modeling tools (NURBS and subdivision surfaces) or move on to animation." Dynamics and effects can come last. "It's all about progression and building a base," he explains. "Maya is huge and ever changing. You'll get nowhere if you don't understand the basics of polys, textures, lights, and cameras. From there, it's up to you."

Rotoscoping is an essential part of Colin's process. "Learn to use rotoscopes when you model... no matter what," says Colin. "It will help you greatly... shoot your rotoscopes from far away with a zoom lens if possible." Using this method minimizes the distortion of perspective and gives you more accurate models. Colin suggests that whenever possible you should use photographs in your textures and—if you have to get really close and the resolution doesn't hold up—you can add a shader as a light bump with some filtering on the image. "Voilà ... no pixelization!" he exclaims. "We actually used this technique a lot on the Egyptian work as the textures were huge and we still had to get in close on them."

Maya's portability and expandability is key. "Everything will plug in to Maya," he explains. "I love this, because I'm not a one-program kind of guy. I like to do some things in this program, some things in that program, and bring it all together in whichever app suits the purpose of the project best. Aside from that, I love Maya's Polygon modeling tools and texturing tools, especially for modeling mechanical or somewhat nonorganic shapes."

Group Bio: Historical Innovation

Company Atlanta Center for IBM e-business Innovation

Location Atlanta, Georgia

Website http://www-1.ibm.com/services/innovation/locatlanta2.shtml

Staff Three Maya artists: Colin Freeman, William Victor, and Brett Gardy

IBM realized that to be successful in the digital economy and e-business it would need to develop a multi-disciplinary approach to application development. The result was the IBM Centers for e-business Innovation, the first of which was launched in Atlanta in 1995. The centers provide a "think-tank" environment for clients to work collaboratively with design experts to innovate and create. The centers' user experience staff comes from the film, television, and recording industries; advertising, brand identity design, and communications agencies; and other multimedia enterprises.

Colin Freeman, William Victor, and Brett Gardy are Lead Media Directors at the Atlanta Center for IBM e-business Innovation. Their responsibilities include leading teams in the design, creation, and implementation of dynamic media content. They each have more than ten years of production experience, creating applications for multimedia and broadcast design studios. They currently specialize in motion graphics; real-time 3D; and interactive applications for the web, CDs, and kiosks.

ten

Digitizing Dream Rides

The crew at Meshwerks *mix their passion for automobiles with cutting-edge 3D technology to bring motorized magic to the worlds of video games, advertising, motion pictures, and television. As the premier producer of high-end 3D automotive models, Meshwerks commands a great deal of respect in the industry. Whether they're doing work for the world's largest automakers or the biggest video-game companies, Meshwerks produces models that set the bar high. Among the many places the Utah-based company's models can be seen are the best-selling Electronic Arts racing simulation* Need for Speed Underground *and the film adaptation of Isaac Asimov's* I Robot.

Building the Digital Garage

In Meshwerks's digital garage, artists use Maya and Photoshop like a professional auto-racing team uses power tools to build a racecar. The days are long, and the deadlines come fast. Meshwerks is headed by lifelong automobile enthusiast, Kevin Scheidle. In the late 1980s and early 1990s, Kevin attended the renowned Art Center College of Design and was a classmate of the celebrated hot-rod designer, Chip Foose. For Kevin, attending Art Center proved a choice of fortunate timing. Although some folks might think of art school as being something other than a high-pressure environment, that's not the case at Art Center. Rather, this Pasadena, California–based school is held in the highest regard in the automotive design world. "Art Center sets high standards," he explains. "You have to eat, drink, and breathe the work." Kevin first learned Alias at Art Center, but instead of using his automotive design knowledge to get a job in the car industry, he fell into the entertainment industry. "Most of the people in the classes were using the early versions of Alias for conceptual automotive and

product design rendering," says Kevin. "I was one of the earliest adopters in the entertainment field." This time period was the infancy of serious computer graphics in Hollywood.

Kevin spent the mid-90s at Viewpoint DataLabs, where he rose through the ranks to Senior Automotive Modeler. In its time, Viewpoint was the industry leader in digital automotive modeling. Once the company was acquired by MetaCreations, however, their focus changed. Kevin left to do freelance work and—after developing solid contacts at the car companies and video-game developers—became so swamped with work that he hired a staff and started his own company. "Things got busy enough to make me decide if I wanted to either turn work away or build the company and hire people," Kevin explains. "At the time, Viewpoint was getting out of the digitizing and modeling business, and they were laying people off. I hired some of the guys that worked at Viewpoint and we went after the work." The venture evolved into Meshwerks, which was formally set up as a corporation in 1999.

Meshwerks bootstrapped as a family business and started out on the Silicon Graphics (SGI) platform. It was a substantial undertaking, considering the costs involved. Meshwerks's first license for Power Animator/Maya version 1 cost approximately $35,000 back in 1998, and the first digitizing arm set the fledgling company back roughly $25,000. Before launching the business, Kevin's dad Mike asked, "What would you need to start up?" When Kevin gave him the numbers, his father cut the first check to buy the SGI workstation, digitizing arm and software. Dad proved a wise investor, as that first investment was paid off in just six months. The company survived six months of slow business after September 11, 2001, and has been growing ever since.

The company's strong reputation for digitizing and modeling has led them to support related specialties, including texture mapping, rigging, rendering, and animation. With a client list that includes automakers DaimlerChrysler, Ford, General Motors, Honda, Nissan, and Toyota; software and game developers such as Electronic Arts, GT Interactive, Infogrames (now Atari), and Microsoft; and advertising agencies such as J. Walter Thompson and Saatchi & Saatchi, Meshwerks has established itself as the best in the business.

Digitizing Cars

Although a good portion of the cars are digitized at Meshwerks's shop in Utah, Kevin and his crew travel frequently to work on cars on location at the world's largest automakers. Whether the road trips take them to Detroit, Europe, or Japan, the scenario is often similar: the Meshwerks crew gains access to the latest and greatest vehicles long before the general public ever gets to cast an eye on them. Over the years, Meshwerks has digitized a good number of factory show cars, as well as the first cars off the production line. Meshwerks often works directly for the auto manufacturer. Other times, they work for game developers, advertising agencies, or movie studios that need digital versions of the cars for games, TV ads, car chases, and the like. Because games can take a year or more to develop, it's essential to digitize the latest cars as early as possible.

Meshwerks automotive digitization workflow starts with raw 3D data. Each car is scanned in sections and pieces. The pieces are stitched together so that everything lines up. Once the pieces are brought into Maya, the original chunks are used a reference template to build new surfaces. As Kevin explains, "We start with the rough stuff from the digitizers, but that raw data is ugly. We make it look pretty once we get it into the workstations. Maya is where all the magic happens." Meshwerks models are renown for their astounding precision, as enabled by Maya. "I have used just about every other 3D program on the planet," says Kevin. "I prefer the intuitive workflow of Maya. It works the way my brain works."

The Ford GT: Digitizing Detroit Muscle

In early spring 2004, Meshwerks was called on to create a digital model of the brand new 200-MPH Ford GT super car. To do so, Kevin and his crew traveled from Utah to Ford's world headquarters in Dearborn, Michigan, where they were granted the honor of digitizing Ford GT #1, the first car off the assembly line. The car was rolled into the studio, and the room was lit for photography work. As with every job, photographs were taken for texture reference, before the car was covered in fingerprints and tape. Figure 10.1 shows the car in a photography cove within the Ford world headquarters.

With the reference photographs taken, the crew began a long process of marking the car with thin body shop tape. The taping process lays out a reference for the digitizing effort. This creates a grid that flows with the lines and shape of the car; the grid is used for visualization and reference in gathering the data. Fine-line plastic-backed masking tape—designed for use in custom paintwork—is used to do most of the taping. The fine-line tape bends and conforms to the curves more readily than paper tape. Conventional ⅛- or ¼-inch masking tape is used for areas that require more adhesion. When a car is symmetrical, it is only necessary to gather data on half the vehicle. Of course, there are always asymmetrical details; antennas, badges, and gas tank doors are some of the most typical. Figure 10.2 shows the front end of the Ford GT with half the car taped out.

The large work is handled using a Portable Coordinate Measuring Machine (CMM) or digitizing arm, while laser scanners are used for detailed data. "Digitizing arms are the

Figure 10.1: The Ford GT #1, ready for digitization

Figure 10.2: The windshield wiper (visible on the right) and the windshield wiper cutout are asymmetrical.

Figure 10.3: The GT in profile with the taping completed

most efficient way to do it," Kevin explains. "The time you save in the modeling phase makes up for the extra time spent in the digitizing process." Over the years, Meshwerks has learned through trial and error, testing all the systems, including lasers and white light. Digitizing arms have won over the other methods, hands down. Figure 10.3 shows Kevin, using the digitizing arm to gather data from the Ford GT's windshield wiper.

The digitizing arm uses articulating joints with sensors. There is a digitizing tip at the end of each arm. The angle of each joint is calculated within the digitizing equipment to report the exact XYZ coordinates of the digitizing tip in space. This information is interpolated to determine the XYZ coordinate of the tip, as it's relative to the base of the arm. "We position the arm to get the most area of the car at one time, in order to produce the maximum area in one file," Kevin explains. "We sample a point every place where the tape lines cross." While the digitizing arms are used for the big data, the smaller areas are handled manually. "In places with more detail such as bolt heads and windshield wipers, we get simplified templates," continues Kevin. "Instead of digitizing everything, we get the general shape and use that to create it from scratch in Maya." Figure 10.4 shows Kevin gathering data from the rocker panel.

Kevin doesn't always stick to the grid. High-resolution data is gathered for reference in complicated sections. The side mirror shown in Figure 10.5 is one example; it had to be freehand scanned for more data. It's always best to gather a generous amount of data points. As Kevin explains, "We can't judge what the final model will look like as we are digitizing, because there will be a lot of refining of data once we get into Maya." The grid provides a basic template. The green tape shown in Figure 10.5 marks out completed sections, to keep track of what has been digitized.

With the main body surfaces of the GT scanned using the digitizing arm, Meshwerks cranked up the laser scanner for gathering the intricate details—pieces that were difficult to capture with the digitizing arm. "On nice big flowing body surfaces, the CMM is the way to go," explains Kevin. "We get what we need and leave the rest." But using the CMM is a

Figure 10.4: Dave Owen, Meshwerks Senior Modeler gets the laser scanner ready, and Kevin uses the CMM, while Mike Scheidle soaks in the beauty of the Ford GT.

Figure 10.5: Kevin with the CMM arm, working on the rocker panel

labor-intensive process. The laser scanner, on the other hand, can gather a million points in one shot in just three or four seconds. On smooth surfaces, this is far too much data. "On something that's highly detailed," Kevin continues. "You can go through and weed out the excess data. For really complex detailed objects, laser is the way to go." Figure 10.6 shows Kevin using the laser scanner on the engine compartment.

Lasers!

Meshwerks has been using their Minolta Vivid 910 laser scanner for almost a year. They've found the Minolta to be compact and easy to travel with and that it provides highly accurate scans (down to microns) in just seconds. The Minolta can capture an area of close to two square meters, within a rectangular aspect ratio (similar to that of TV). It's so precise that it can scan a dime and get surface detail with impressions.

There was plenty of data for the laser scanner to gather in the Ford GT's engine compartment—from the triangulated aluminum frame members to the 5.4 liter MOD V-8 engine and coil-over suspension. Although the engine is similar in some respect to engines used in other high-performance Fords, the GT engine uses a new all-aluminum block with a specially modified supercharger and water-air intercooler to reach 500 horsepower. Figure 10.7 provides a better view of the engine compartment.

So how fast is the Ford GT? Plenty fast! *Car and Driver* magazine clocked 0–60 mph in just 3.3 seconds and a blistering quarter mile in11.6 seconds.

Figure 10.6: The laser scanner was used to scan the engine compartment, wheels, and gas cap, among other pieces.

Figure 10.7: Can you say "supercharger?"

Once the gear is packed up, the laptops are packed with data. All the information is uploaded to Meshwerks servers before the team leaves, and team members in Utah often begin working on the project before the road crew returns home. With the raw data in hand, the serious work begins. The scans must be matched together into one big file that is used as a template to build the actual model, largely using the polygons and NURBS tools in Maya. The resulting geometry ends up as subdivision surfaces.

Most of the photography is taken for modeling and texturing reference. This allows the modelers to know which surfaces are shiny, which are polished, and which have a matte finish. Tire sidewalls are often photographed for use as high-resolution texture maps and to generate bump maps in Photoshop. The bump maps make the sidewall lettering appear as if it's sticking out of the surface of the sidewall. This adds depth to the lettering and other markings. Photographs of the various badges, decals, and stickers are either re-created or retouched in Photoshop. These are applied as textures in Maya. The actual logo and script are built with geometry.

The Ford GT was digitized in just two days. Although models for hot projects can be completed in this time frame, it normally takes four or five days. Once the data comes into Maya, one modeler usually handles the job. If the process needs to be sped up, pieces can be broken out of the process—badges, wheels, door handles, and the like—and these individual components can be farmed out to additional modelers. One person needs to do the body panels, however, to ensure that the panels are consistent and match without any glitches. The completed model on a meticulous job—one with a great deal of interior, exterior, headlight, and taillight niceties—can take three or four weeks. Details in engine, interior, and under the front hood racks up additional time. For car lovers, this is a dream job. Figure 10.8 shows the Ford GT project road crew: Dimitri Bourdos, Mike Scheidle, Kevin Scheidle, and Dave Owen with Ford GT #1. It's all about the perks!

*Figure 10.8:
Dimitri, Mike,
Kevin, and Dave
in their new
Ford GT shirts
with the real car*

Company Bio: Meshwerks Power Drive

Company Meshwerks

Location South Jordan, Utah

Website: www.meshwerks.com/

Staff Seven employees, plus contractors

Founded 1999

Meshwerks is a 3D digital-content creation studio with clients in the film, commercial, broadcast television, and game industries. The company specializes in digital auto reconstruction, relying on extremely detailed scanning, modeling, and texturing. It also provides rigging, animation, and rendering, as well as project pipeline development.

The Nissan 350Z: Interior Details

Most of the cars that Meshwerks models include a simplified upper interior—often referred to as a silhouette or shadow interior. The silhouette interior is intended to show that there's *something* there, but it's not a high-detail model; rather, it's done in a medium resolution. On occasion, however, Meshwerks is called on to do high-resolution interiors. The Nissan 350Z shown in Figure 10.9 is a fabulous example of Meshwerks interior handiwork and represents one of the most complex interior models that the crew has completed to date in Maya.

Interior work presents special challenges. Gathering data and getting into all the nooks and crannies require a lot of patience and flexibility. And there's a mechanical aspect to it, as well; seats may need to be removed during the data acquisition process. All in all, it's a lot of work. "I have freehand scanned complete interiors," explains Kevin. "You have to be a contortionist. Interiors are so much more intricate and filled with detail." Meshwerks now forgoes the digitizing arm for interiors, in favor of the laser.

Producing an interior model can take two to three times longer than an exterior model. Before switching to the laser for interior work, Meshwerks spent as much as a week digitizing an interior with the CMM. "More than just the computer power and software knowledge, this is grueling physical labor," Kevin continues "It takes its toll on you. It's almost like your doing some kind of crazy automotive yoga." Figure 10.10 provides two more views of the Nissan 350Z interior, which Dimitri painstakingly digitized and modeled over a six-week period. The final model weighs in at a whopping 1.5 million polygons.

Figure 10.9: The interior modeling on the Nissan 350Z was not done for a client; rather, it was undertaken solely to showcase Meshwerks capabilities.

Figure 10.10: This rendering of the Nissan 350Z shows a gray shader on the interior.

World's Fastest Growing High-End 3D Auto Model Catalog

Once models are created, Meshwerks owns them. As the artist, the company reserves the right to resell the models, unless a contract states that a model cannot be resold. Although some projects are confidential and cannot be resold, most of the work that Meshwerks has produced over the years is available for purchase from Meshwerks.com

The EleMENTAL Woodie

Back in Chapter 1, I introduced you to the chopped-and-woodified Honda Element. What started out as a crazy late-night idea quickly took shape as a digital reality after we first contacted Meshwerks. Dave Owen, is the man responsible for taking the digital torch to an existing Honda Element model in Maya. He chopped six inches out of the top and widened the roof to accommodate the chop. The suspension was slammed to the ground with a serious drop. Wood panels frame the front and suicide doors, in a style that pays homage to the 1946 Ford.

The team started by rendering their stock Honda Element, making prints that they drew over. This gave them some rough ideas of what was possible. They soon decided which direction to take. Just like the real world: you start the project with a pencil in hand, not a torch. Lowering the digital Element wasn't difficult—rather, it was just a matter of translating the whole car. The serious modifications began with the top chop. "I grabbed every one of the vertices on the top and dragged it down," explains Dave. "I had to lengthen the front of the roof for the angle to match up with the front pillars, and I had to widen the roof to make it

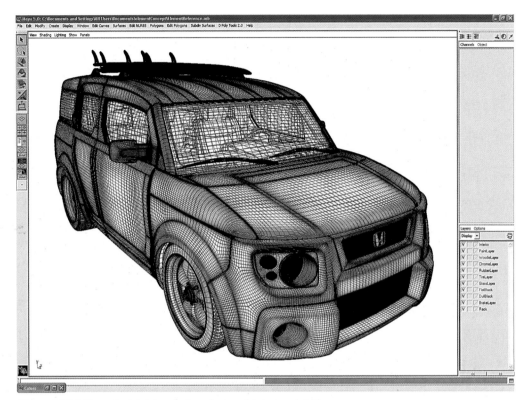

Figure 10.11 Note the high level of surface and interior details.

match the sides." Once the changes were made to the sheet metal, everything fit tightly. Figure 10.11 shows the Woodie in a three-quarter wireframe front view.

It takes a sweet set of tires and rims to really set off a special ride, and the EleMENTAL Woodie is no exception. Our wicked little custom rolls on Pirelli tires, wrapped around 20-inch American Racing Torq-Thrust II rims. The rear wheels are shod with massive Pirelli PZero Rosso Asimmetricos, and the front wheels are fitted with Pirelli PZero Rosso Direzionales. Notice the extreme detail in the tire tread in Figure 10.12.

Brembo brakes haul the EleMENTAL Woodie down at all four corners, with sharp-looking rotors. The brakes and tires were scavenged from an existing Lamborghini model, while Dave modeled the wheels from scratch. Figure 10.13 shows a close-up view of a wheel and brake combo.

Take a look at a wireframe view of the wheel, tire, and brake assembly, as shown in Figure 10.14. The tire tread construction demonstrates Meshwerks fanatical attention to detail. Although some shops might be content to simply texture map the tread, Meshwerks's construction of tread geometry puts this model over the top.

The EleMENTAL Woodie is a truly high-end 3D model, built with excruciating attention to detail. "We model everything for projects like this that will be used at super high resolution in a print image," explains Dave. "There are more than a million polys in this model. The grill is all built with geometry. The tires have real tread. The disk brake rotors have real holes. There are vertical grooves in the headlights." Meshwerks knows that in these situations there can be no cheating with textures. It's all built into the model.

Figure 10.12: The tread of the Pirelli PZero tires is not a texture map—it is completely modeled.

Figure 10.13: The work on the wheels, tires, and brakes is quite impressive.

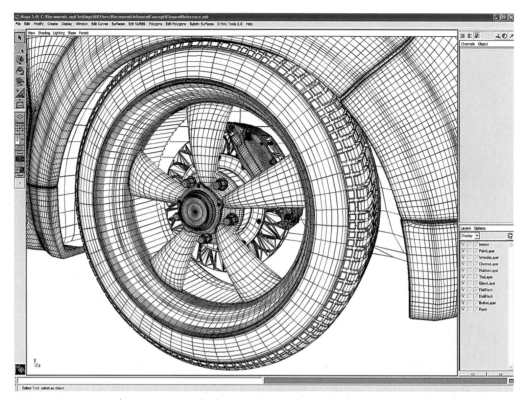

Figure 10.14: A wireframe view reveals the complexity of the wheel, tire, and brake combo.

Creating the woodie panels took a good bit of time and some handiwork in Photoshop. "I initially found a site that made aftermarket woodie kits that covered just the lower door," explains Dave. "After we looked at them, we decided that the doors would look much better with wood encasing the windows." Using a 1946 Ford Woodie as inspiration, Dave built the extruded wood panels with two different wood textures. The doors are covered with red-stained Philippine mahogany and framed with hard rock maple, capturing a classic Woodie look. The extrusion gives the wood panels the proper amount of depth, heading off the dreaded contact paper wood-grain look so common to psuedo-woodies. The wood-grain textures were altered with Photoshop's Variations to create the proper tones. "Whenever I texture, I go to Photoshop," says Dave. "I never touch any other program."

The team originally planned to continue the wood paneling onto the front fender and back quarter panel, but decided against this approach. The wood solely on the door frames creates a clean, classic effect. To help clean up the sides of the Element, the lower body cladding—which comes from the factory in bare gray plastic—was shaded with the body color in Maya. To further enhance the Woodie's custom look, the door handles have been shaved (removed) and replaced by electronic door openers. Figure 10.15 shows the clean effect of painting the lower body cladding.

Figure 10.15: The Woodie's painted cladding is a big improvement over the stock Element.

Final renders of the EleMENTAL Woodie were created at GTN, Inc. (www.gtninc.com/), a high-end postproduction house headquartered in Detroit, Michigan. The rendering work was completed by GTN's Keith Johnston.

The front of the Element received a good bit of attention as well. The eye is immediately drawn to the headlamps, which started their life attached to a Ford F-150. (It certainly helps to have a catalog full of digitized cars to grab parts from!) Body-color bezels lend a unique look to the headlamps, while the nose was cleaned up substantially over the stock model, as shown in Figure 10.16.

As with the side cladding, the bare gray plastic has been painted with the body color. Magnificently intricate yet elegantly simple upper and lower tube grills complete the look. Figure 10.17 shows a head-on view of the grills. You can almost smell the bug cleaner!

Figure 10.18 provides a view of the EleMENTAL Woodie complete with surfboards in wireframe, as seen from above. Why create a new surfboard from scratch when all you have to do is build a new texture map?

Figure 10.16: Close-up view of the custom headlamp assembly

Figure 10.17: The grills were created from individual chrome tubes.

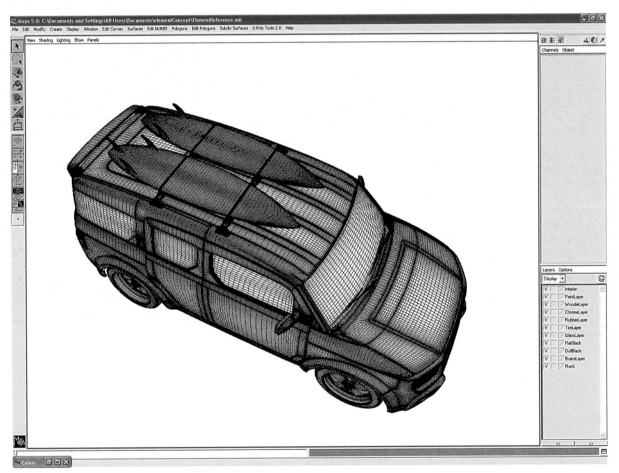

Figure 10.18: Build one surfboard, and you've built them all.

Figure 10.19: Everybody's gone surfin'!

Up top, chrome racks and a rear sunroof add visual interest. And what woodie would be complete without a couple of surfboards lashed to the roof? The EleMENTAL is no exception. Dave added the surfboards shown in Figure 10.19 to great effect.

Artist Bio: Dave Owen, Senior Modeler

Dave Owen (www.davenowen.com) is the man responsible for modifying Meshwerks's Element model (which was initially created for Honda's fabulously successful Element television commercial in which the boxy SUV is built from Lego blocks). Although the story of how I hooked up with Meshwerks to build the EleMENTAL Woodie might make a good sidebar, the story of how Dave came to Meshwerks surely does too.

After some multimedia exposure and Photoshop from high school, Dave attended the Vancouver Institute of Media Arts (VanArts), in Vancouver, completing the one year VanArts computer animation program. Dave worked intensively at VanArts, putting in 60 hours a week.

Just 21, Dave has been with Meshwerks since 2003, starting as a freelance modeler. Landing at Meshwerks proved most fortunate for an admitted total car nut. "You have to be pretty passionate about it," says Dave. "I'm happy with what I do and can see the fruits of my labor. My demo reel was all car models. I've always wanted to do special effects with cars."

Meshwerks Game Ventures

Meshwerks has contributed 3D models and animation work for a number of top-shelf video games. Although the company is best known for automotive modeling, its expertise extends to character modeling, texturing, and animation. Over the years, Meshwerks has worked on a wide range of titles including Electronic Arts's *Need for Speed Underground*, *Freekstyle*, *Lord of the Rings*, and the *Tiger Woods* golf series.

Need for Speed Underground

Electronic Arts's *Need for Speed Underground* is the hottest racing sim released in 2003, and a game designed to appeal to the tuner at heart. Players start with a stock base model car and street race to earn prestige and money. The more races you win, the more money you make … which you'll promptly plow into tricking out your ride with hop-up equipment. The game lets you change your ride's appearance, starting with different paint, graphics, decals, and window tint. As you earn more cash, you'll swap out hoods, bumpers, spoilers, and rims. The main focus of the game isn't just the *appearance* of your street machine, it's the *performance*. Savvy racers swap out computers, exhausts, suspensions, and brakes. And, of course, you can bolt on everyone's favorite go-fast pieces such as turbochargers and nitrous oxide injection systems. With hundreds of aftermarket parts from more than 50 suppliers—including Koni, NOS, Sparco, and Momo—you'll take your stock vehicle to totally tricked-out crazy land.

It might be a bit much to say that the racing action is highly realistic (when in reality it's way-over-the-top cool), but it's no stretch to say that it's simply amazing. Despite the wild nature of the game, you'll feel as if you're in the race. This is due, in no small part, to the highly accurate 3D car models and snappy accessories. Meshwerks produced a number of the 3D models in *Need for Speed Underground*, including the Nissan 350Z, Mazda Miata, Mitsubishi Lancer, and the VW Golf GTI. The game shipped in November 2003 and is available for the PlayStation 2, Microsoft Xbox, Nintendo GameCube, and PC.

Need for Speed Underground is highly addictive. It is a black hole of time and will swallow your life and that of those around you.

Freekstyle

Meshwerks provided both character and motorcycle rigging for Electronic Arts's *Freekstyle*. Crave the virtual smell of dirt and gasoline? Can't get enough big air? Fill up your Freekout Meter and bury the needle, and you can pull off a "Super Sick Trick." Rated E (for Everyone), Freekstyle shipped in mid-2002 and is available for both the PlayStation 2 and Nintendo GameCube. *Freekstyle* is a stunt-centric freestyle motorcross game, in the style of EA's highly popular SSX snowboarding game—lots of big air, crazy tricks, and snappy wisecracks, along with great game play and wicked cool animation.

IGN.com lathered praise on the game: "The production is extremely high, the game play is intense, incredible, and challenging, and the graphics are both over-the-top and downright beautiful." *Freekstyle* features a total of eight crazy freestyle motocrossers: Mike Metzger, Brian Deegan, Leeann Tweeden, Stefy Bau, Clifford "The Flying Hawaiian" Adoptante, Mad Mike Jones, Jessica Patterson, and Greg "Albee" Albertyn. All the riders have their own unique motorcycles and equipment.

eleven

Mirko Ilić: A Body of Work in 3D

Famed New York–based designer

Mirko Ilić has been at the forefront of 3D design since the early 1990s. Mirko's work for newspapers such as the New York Times, Los Angeles Times, *and the* Village Voice, *for magazines such as* BusinessWeek, Newsweek, National Geographic, *and* Rolling Stone, *and many other publications never shies from the controversial. And Mirko is not content to work only in the field of editorial illustration. Mirko's career also spans the worlds of graphic design, animation, and interactivity. His design portfolio includes countless posters, book covers, and music CD art. His motion picture work includes title sequences for the hit Meg Ryan/Tom Hanks romantic comedy* You've Got Mail *(1998) and the Alec Baldwin/Bill Murray short* Scout's Honor *(1999). This chapter takes a different tack than the previous chapters. Here, I opted not to deconstruct a handful of pieces, in favor of providing a larger overview of Mirko's methodology with a gallery of his recent work in Maya and Photoshop.*

A Time-Tested Methodology

Mirko has a unique collaborative design process. It all starts out, as he explains it, when he has "a vision of the illustration." Working in collaboration with Maya artist Lauren DeNapoli, Mirko creates a marker comp to start, which he gives to Lauren. The two discuss the idea, and Lauren sets off to create the initial scene. "We have been working together for such a long time," explains Lauren. "I have a good idea of his aesthetic. I know what he wants." When the preliminary image is approved, Lauren comes back with a rendered version. Then, Lauren and Mirko experiment with the renders a bit, playing with the image by moving things around, as well as changing lighting and camera angles. Once the final rendering is complete, Mirko converts it from RGB to CMYK in Photoshop and gets the image ready for process printing. He touches up the images as necessary and handles any color correction. Some retouching may also be involved at this point.

The following gallery pages reproduce some of the finest examples of the studio's recent editorial illustration work completed with Maya and Photoshop.

Figure 11.1: The camouflaged dog in Scent of War *has eyes for Iraq.*

Scent of War

Art Director Minh Uong

Client *The Village Voice*

With a Halloween-colored background of black oil rigs starkly silhouetted against an orange sky, *Scent of War* takes on a frightening air. With the scent of war in the air, the camouflaged dog hungrily eyes the Iraq map-covered bone as its image is reflected in the pool of oil that covers the desert floor. Lauren built all the geometry in the image in Maya. The dog's camouflaged coat was created as a procedural texture with solid fractals layered on top of each other. The map of Iraq originally came from a scanned image and was projected as a texture map onto the bone. Raytracing provides the reflectivity in the oil.

America's Other Drug Problem

Art Director Jose Fernandez

Client *Men's Health*

The sinister wind-up tin doctor in *America's Other Drug Problem* strikes fear where there should be hope—the fear being that prescription medicine is fast becoming a drug problem for society. The startlingly realistic toy looks both convincing and evil as it marches forward, prescription bottle in hand. Dramatic lighting bathes the tin doctor in an evil red glow, as it casts a looming shadow. As Lauren explains, "The spotlights and simple red light add to the whole evil vibe."

Figure 11.2: The wind-up doctor in America's Other Drug Problem *has an evil vibe.*

Figure 11.3: The egg carton car in What Price Safety? *makes you wonder about safety on the road.*

Figure 11.4: Eyeballs at the movies in Take Three *munch on popcorn while soaking up the big screen.*

What Price Safety?

Art Director Alice Cheung

Client *BusinessWeek*

The egg-carton car in *What Price Safety?* displays its precious cargo, each shoulder-belt strapped into its seat. The editorial piece concerned new automotive safety features. A dark orange background provides good contrast against the nicely textured tan carton. The project's topic and time frame demanded rapid innovation and repurposing. "I built the egg carton from scratch," explains Lauren. "Then I took wheels from a car model and added them to the carton." The egg carton texture is a solid fractal with a little variation. The image was produced in roughly half a day

Take Three

Art Director Minh Uong

Client *The Village Voice*

In this piece for the Third Annual Village Voice Film Critics' Poll, an audience of eyeballs in *Take Three* is fixated at the projection screen that hangs above and behind the viewer's head. With popcorn, sodas, and candy in hand, the eyeballs focus on the action while the beam from the projector casts a spectacular effect. The eyeball-people were modeled with subdivision surfaces and rigged. Lauren painted the texture map of the eyes in different colors, using a layered shader to gain the appearance of a shiny eyeball. The main lighting uses a spot with fog, which makes the light break into separate rays, thus achieving the darkened theater look. An ambient light lends additional glow. The eyeballs show subtle reflection maps and highlights. The popcorn was created from a sphere that Lauren "totally ripped apart in different directions."

Special Section on Intelligence

Art Director Gigi Fava

Client *The New York Times*

The startling *Special Section on Intelligence* piece mixes sepia tones with brilliant pseudo X-ray imagery for an article on security. The scanning machine was built from scratch in Maya, using photographic references. The skeletons of the

Figure 11.5: The X-ray image effect in Special Section on Intelligence *provides an eerie reminder of the security-crazed times in which we live.*

travelers and security workers are shown suspended in their respective transparent bodies to portray a world in which intelligence and security have increasing importance. Lauren modeled the skeletons inside the people, using different layers. "I parented each bone in the skeletons to each Maya bone to make it easier to pose," Lauren explains. "This avoids hand placing each bone. Using a rigged skeleton made it go a little bit faster. Anything with a character takes longer … modeling reality takes time." The original image had a black background and light-blue image, like a traditional film X ray. Mirko inverted the image in Photoshop to create the sepia tone.

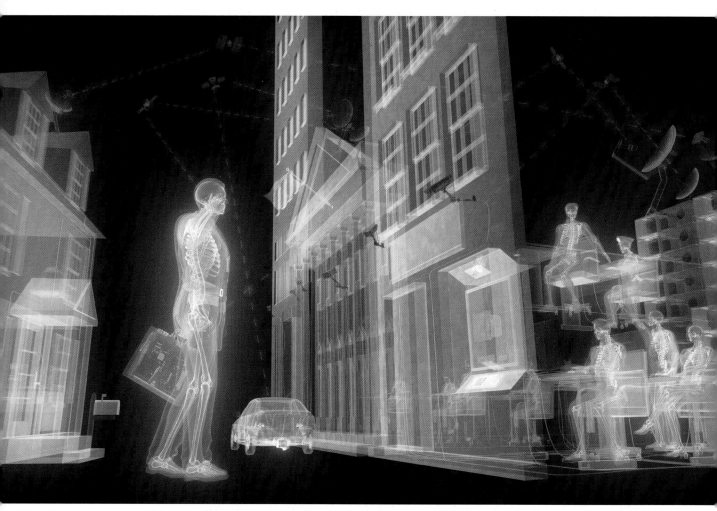

Figure 11.6: Mirko's first X-ray image proved so popular that National Geographic *commissioned him to produce* Data Trial.

Data Trial

Art Director Jeff Osborn

Client *National Geographic*

Mirko's first X-ray piece created quite a stir and prompted many a phone call. "The military was thinking I had some special machine," exclaims Mirko. A run on X-ray art soon ensued. Mirko's second X-ray–effect piece (for *National Geographic*), *Data Trial,* forgoes a monochrome palette for a more graphic approach of black, red, and ghostly blue. Satellites beam data about the skies as security workers keep track of every move. The piece warns that your actions are being monitored more than you will ever know.

Absolut Times

Art Director Richard Press

Client *The New York Times, Times Talk*

The ingenious web printing press in *Absolut Times* uses vodka bottles as press cylinders. The front page of the *New York Times* is shown snaking through the Web, with marvelous ray-traced reflections on the bottle/cylinders. With the instant familiarity of the Absolut advertising series, this image uses basic 3D geometry and spotlights to great dramatic effect.

Figure 11.8: The dragon in China Breaks Out *was modified from an existing DAZ model.*

China Breaks Out

Art Director Leah Purcell

Client *Newsweek*

In *China Breaks Out,* the Chinese dragon breaking out of its golden shell seems to signify China's emergence as a world power. The dragon is a DAZ Productions (**www.daz3d.com**) model that Lauren modified to fit the Chinese theme and placed in the egg. The egg started out as a simple sphere in Maya. Lauren cut the hole (in the shape of China), did an offset, and extruded the egg along the trim line. Mirko provided the map for the egg, which was then textured, reflection mapped, and raytraced.

Justice Turns on Her Cams

Art Director Steven Heller

Client *The New York Times Sunday Book Review*

The video cameras that adorn Justice's head in *Justice Turns on Her Cams* signify the stark realities of the world after September 11, 2001. Although justice may be blind, the government has new authority to watch what people do and to interfere with those actions. Justice is lit with a spotlight from above, bringing shimmering highlights to the model. A gold shader, reflection maps, and raytracing combine to provide a convincingly realistic effect. Using fog and glow to enhance the cast shadows, the spotlights impart a dramatic look. Lauren modeled the clothing, blindfold, sword, scales of justice, and security cameras in Maya.

Figure 11.9: The camcorders in Justice Turns on Her Cams *make it clear: we are being watched.*

Writing Science

Art Director Carol Kaufman

Client *Los Angeles Times Book Review*

Full of stars, the bottle of ink in *Writing Science* portrays time, space, and the texture of reality. Puddles of texture-mapped star-filled ink are strewn about the stark white desktop. The ink drips out of the bottle and covers the tip of the pen nib. The pen shaft makes great use of a shiny metallic shader. The shadows fall close to the bottle of ink and pen, suggesting a light high overhead. But perhaps the most intriguing feature is the ink bottle itself; its reflective glass provides a fantastic distortion of the planets and stars.

Figure 11.10: The bottle of ink in Writing Science *is full of the wonders of the universe.*

Portrait of Rob Malda

Art Director Gail Anderson

Client *Rolling Stone*

In *Portrait of Rob Malda*, the Slashdot founder's face is shown as a montage of translucent 0s and 1s. CmdrTaco, as Rob is known on Slashdot.com, created a highly-influential community website that serves as a virtual water-cooler for the Internet's techie elite. The hovering flutter of 0s and 1s seems to say that the data makes the man, and vice versa. Texture mapping on the central digits defines the face, while the outer digits fade into the dark background. Green and cyan highlights show on the edges of selected digits to great dramatic effect. The green lighting highlights the edges of the T-shirt, providing a visual clue to the backlit light source.

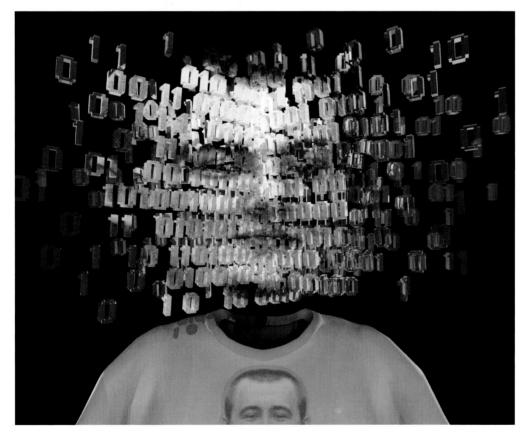

Figure 11.11: Portrait of Rob Malda *shows what the Slash-dot founder is made of.*

Drilling in Alaska

Art Director Ron Gabriel

Client *New York Times Upfront*

Drilling in Alaska jams a whimsical drink umbrella and red-and-white barbershop pole-striped drinking straw into the politically touchy subject of drilling for oil in the Alaskan

Figure 11.12: The oil cocktail in Drilling in Alaska *is a potent concoction.*

wilderness. As with Mirko's *Scent of War,* raytracing on the oil spot delivers convincingly realistic reflections and texture. The balmy tropical print texture-mapped onto the crinkly tissue-paper umbrella contrasts with the frozen surroundings. The photographic background of the snow-covered mountains fades a bit in the distance through a touch of atmospheric fog. The crisp gradient sky and the 3D-rendered cocktail combine to slap the viewer into recognition of the environmental quandary.

The Last Taboo

Art Director Carol Kaufman

Client *Los Angeles Times Book Review*

With its brilliantly elegant and purely black-and-white approach, *The Last Taboo* tackles the touchy subject of interracial marriages. The stark graphic background suggests the ebony and ivory of a piano, as the arms simultaneously lift from the page and fade into their respective keys. Careful bump mapping and lighting serve to bring this piece into the third dimension. Skin, bone, and vein textures are readily apparent. Bright white lighting burns out the highlights of the white arm, while providing subtle detail to the black arm.

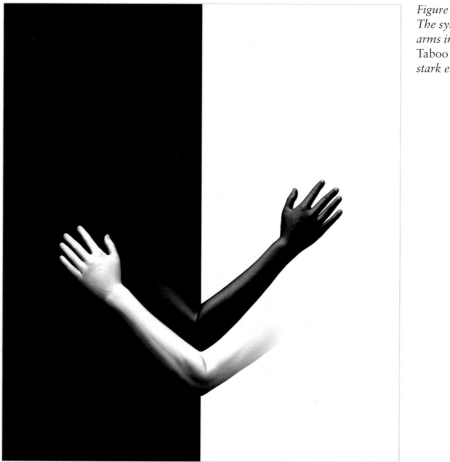

Figure 11.13: The symmetrical arms in The Last Taboo *deliver stark elegance.*

Figure 11.14: Mirko's International *possesses an overwhelming quality of sheer size.*

International

Art Director Mirko Ilić

Client International Design Center

The International Design Center gave three artists each a different word to create a design piece. Mirko's highly graphic piece, *International,* is shown in Figure 11.14. The grid of words seems to run forever, with harsh lighting and strong shadows that suggest a huge structure spread across the horizon at noon on a hot summer day. Dueling warm and cool gray tones lock together with the harsh light of the sun almost directly overhead. The word grid appears free of textures, relying only on solid tones for maximum graphic impact.

Connect

Creative Director Don Morris

Art Director Josh Klenert

Client King Fish Media

In *Connect*, Mirko provides his take on the subject of security on the Internet. Created for a client of King Fish Media (a Salem, Massachusetts-based marketing firm) the startlingly elegant barbed-wire computer floats over the stark-white desktop. The translucent blue screen hovers in the monitor space, as a vertical strand of barbed wire shows through. Not only is the computer built of barbed wire, but the Internet connection and mouse cable are, as well. The thinly cast shadows hammer home the point. If only our computers were this impervious to nasty virus infections and infestations of heinous spyware, the world would be a better place.

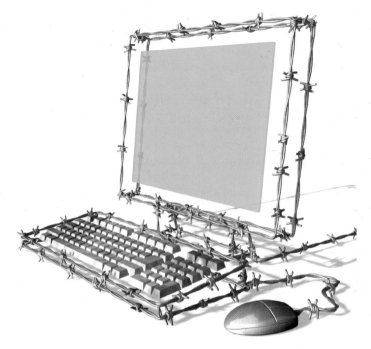

Figure 11.15: The barbed-wire computer in Connect *floats in space.*

Bio: Mirko Ilić

Mirko Ilić is a highly accomplished New York City–based artist and designer. His extensive work in the worlds of graphic design and 3D have won accolades from around the globe. Mirko's work has appeared in the *New York Times, Los Angeles Times, Village Voice, National Geographic, Rolling Stone,* and many other high-profile publications. He was art director of Time Magazine's International Editions and the New York Times op-ed pages. See more of his work at **www.mirkoilic.com**.

Forced to Fight

Art Director Minh Uong

Client *The Village Voice*

With *Forced to Fight,* Mirko provides food for thought, as young New Yorkers debate the draft. Clad in an oversized helmet, dog tags, night-vision glasses, and a diaper, the baby looks at the viewer with a tear in his eye and a massive automatic rifle in his lap. The desert camouflage on the helmet serves to put the piece in geographic context. The bump mapping and metallic shader on the dog tags provide a convincing effect, while the lighting makes the dog tag chain glow with a harsh light. With its oil-painted appearance, the baby's skin falls somewhere between realistic and toylike. The gunstock, however, looks menacingly real. Subtle red lighting touches the right side surfaces, as if to warn of the impending heat of battle. An Alpha channel layer was created for the skin in Maya. The skin layer was duplicated in Photoshop and blurred with 30% opacity—with the exception of the tear—to give a gentle glow to the skin. The tear was left sharp for contrast.

Figure 11.16: Forced to Fight *delivers a powerful message.*

Bio: Lauren DeNapoli

Lauren DeNapoli is a self-taught Maya artist. In the early 1990s, Lauren was a student at the School of Visual Arts (SVA) in New York City. At SVA, Lauren started with painting and sculpting, but soon got interested in computer graphic design and Photoshop. Lauren was introduced to the world of 3D design while working for an offset printing company. "There was nowhere to learn 3D back then, so I read all the books I could find," she explains. "Then SVA began offering some classes." Lauren started out with Wavefront, running on a Silicon Graphics Indy workstation.

After graduating from SVA, Lauren worked at an architectural firm doing 3D visualizations before landing at MPC, a NYC-based computer graphics value-added-reseller. MPC hired Lauren to work as an Alias instructor and demo specialist. Fate struck when Mirko bought a computer from MPC just as Lauren was looking to get back into production.

On Producing with Maya

When Mirko first set out in the world of 3D art, it was an incredibly pricey business. Mirko's first Silicon Graphics workstation set him back $75,000 in 1991. For the first few years, Mirko's design studio used Softimage. After Mirko's wife had a baby, his career priorities changed as he steered away from 3D design and switched to 2D work, largely using Photoshop. But Mirko couldn't stay away from 3D, and he began using form Z and Electronic Image. Soon Mirko found it was "time to grow up and do something different. That's how I ended up with Alias."

The workflow afforded by the 3D world allows Mirko's studio to quickly produce world-class artwork on increasingly tight deadlines. "We have a large database of categorized models that makes it convenient to recycle them for future pieces," Mirko explains, "though there are many occasions that the subject requires specific models to be built." And the constant innovation in Maya has brought productivity gains and creative freedom, as well. "Paint Effects has made the biggest impact on the way we work," reveals Mirko. "It's great for making quick texture maps or actual geometry. It has really enhanced our illustrations."

Index

Note to the Reader: Throughout this index **boldfaced** page numbers indicate primary discussions of a topic. *Italicized* page numbers indicate illustrations.

After Effects® and Photoshop®:
Animation and Production Effects for DV and Film

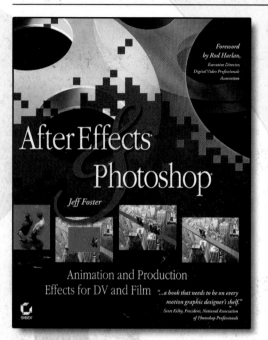

By Jeff Foster
ISBN: 0-7821-4317-2
US $49.99

If you're in the business of motion graphics or desktop digital video production, you know that Adobe's After Effects and Photoshop are two of the most indispensable content creation tools. More integrated than ever before, the world's number-one compositing and image-editing programs can be used in tandem to create quality work at a relatively low cost. But it takes years of experience to figure out how to get the most out of this remarkable duo.

With *After Effects and Photoshop: Animation and Production Effects for DV and Film*, graphics guru Jeff Foster has created the first book devoted to showing how you can use these two programs together to produce animations and effects on the desktop. This practical guide focuses exclusively on techniques commonly used in the field as well as cutting-edge production tricks. These hands-on projects will demystify cool Hollywood effects and help you solve your daily challenges. And they'll inspire you to think more artistically when approaching your creations.

Inside, you'll discover pro techniques for motion graphics and video production, including how to:

- *Add depth and realism to your animations by mimicking real motion*
- *Use exaggerated movements to enhance characterization*
- *Apply 3-D animation to 2-D images*
- *Remove background fodder with blue-screen garbage mattes*
- *Employ rotoscoping techniques for frame-by-frame retouching*
- *Construct realistic composites and scene locations using matte painting techniques*
- *Make movies from stills by simulating 3-D camera motion*
- *Utilize perspective, speed, and scale to create believable moving objects*
- *Produce realistic special effects such as noise, clouds, and smoke*
- *Practice imaginative motion titling effects that grab people's attention*
- *Develop professional scene transitions using 3-D layer animations*
- *And much more!*

SYBEX®
www.sybex.com